THROUGH THE BURNING STEPPE

ELENA KOZHINA

TRANSLATED BY
VADIM MAHMOUDOV

RIVERHEAD BOOKS
New York

THROUGH THE BURNING STEPPE

A Memoir of Wartime Russia, 1942–1943

Most Riverhead Books are available at special quantity discounts for bulk purchases for sales promotions, premiums, fund-raising, or educational use. Special books, or book excerpts, can also be created to fit specific needs.

For details, write: Special Markets, The Berkley Publishing Group, 375 Hudson Street, New York, New York 10014.

RIVERHEAD BOOKS
Published by The Berkley Publishing Group
A division of Penguin Putnam Inc.
375 Hudson Street
New York, New York 10014

First Riverhead hardcover edition: March 2000
First Riverhead trade paperback edition: March 2001
Riverhead trade paperback ISBN: 1-57322-855-9

The Penguin Putnam Inc. World Wide Web site address is
http://www.penguinputnam.com

The Library of Congress has catalogued
the Riverhead hardcover edition as follows:

Kozhina, Elena Fedorovna.
Through the burning steppe : a wartime memoir / by Elena
Kozhina ; translated by Vadim Mahmoudov.
p. cm.
ISBN 1-57322-153-8
1. Kozhina, Elena Fedorovna. 2. World War, 1939–1945—
Personal narratives, Russian. 3. World War, 1939–1945—
Refugees. 4. World War, 1939–1945—Soviet Union.
5. Children—Soviet Union—Biography. I. Title.
D811.5+
940.54'47—dc21
99-053356 CIP

PRINTED IN THE UNITED STATES OF AMERICA

10 9 8 7 6 5 4 3 2 1

ACKNOWLEDGMENTS

Before the first page of this book, I wish to acknowledge with gratitude the people who helped it see the light of day:

my literary agent, Thomas Colchie, who exhibited miracles of professional energy, introducing many people to the manuscript of an unknown author and making its publication possible;

my son, Vadim Mahmoudov, who translated it into English, the language of a country which hospitably accepted our family during a very difficult period of our lives;

Dr. Roberta Reeder, who read my manuscript, both in the original Russian and in English. I was deeply touched by the attention she showed to this text;

and finally, my husband, Alexei Mahmoudov.

Elena Kozhina
New York
October 4, 1999

THROUGH THE BURNING STEPPE

GERMAN TROOPS OCCUPIED our Cossack village on July 31, 1942. It was the eve of my birthday; the next day, I would be nine years old.

For the entire day we walked through the steppe, retreating. By now, "we" included only me and Mama. We were the only ones left alive.

Five months before, in February, the five of us had boarded a cattle train full of evacuated Leningraders after a journey through the "Road of Life," across frozen Lake Ladoga. At each stop, our railcar became roomier as the dead were carried out. At the Cherepovets stop, the body of my older brother, Vadik, was carried out. He did not live to his tenth birthday. There were no coffins; the emaciated bodies were simply put on stretchers and taken away to mass graves. Mama covered Vadik with a blanket.

"Take the blanket back," someone said quietly. "The living could use it."

"But what about him . . ." Mama did not finish. But also did not take the blanket back. As if it could still warm her first-born. Or as if there were no longer any divide between him, the dead, and us, the half-living.

And there really was no divide. We all were getting weaker each day; food was no longer helping. At each stop, the railcar doors rolled open with a bang, and people carrying stretchers would peek inside.

"You got anybody?" they would ask.

Someone by the door would point toward a corner. "There. Take him."

"What, you don't even have a sheet to cover him?" the medic would ask disapprovingly as he approached a dead old man stretched out on the wooden floor.

"He's not mine. All his kin are dead, he's the last one. I would give my own sheet, but I'm too weak to get up—there it is, in the bag. Why not take it? I'm the last one, too; tomorrow they'll come for me. If we stay here until morning, you'll be the one coming for me."

Indeed, the train stopped sometimes for an hour, sometimes for a day. Nobody knew where it was headed, when and how long it would stop. Sometimes it stopped in the middle of empty fields or naked, leafless forests. Sometimes it stopped at a junction full of military echelons and other trains carrying coal. There it would be met by women with knapsacks of bread, eggs, boiled potatoes, salted pickles. They sold them unwillingly, often bartering them for the Leningraders' belongings. Mama desperately tried to buy anything we asked for. "We" were me and my three-year-old sister, Tanya; Grandma never asked for anything. She was already very weak and spoke little.

The train kept going and going, helplessly and senselessly, without a schedule, without a destination, like a leaf floating down a drying creek. Left behind was Lake Ladoga, frozen, it seemed, forever. Ahead were the scorching front lines, with German divisions pouring through them. The train was headed toward the front, and quite a few times we found ourselves under attack by bombers, just as in Leningrad.

At the Kuschevka stop, eighty kilometers from Rostov, we could go no farther. The roads were cut off, the railways had been ground up by bombing raids, and the front was approaching us now much faster than we were retreating from Lake Ladoga.

They settled us in the hut of an old Cossack woman. A cart took us to the gateway. Mama carried Tanya in her arms. Grandma and I thought that we could walk ourselves. As it turned out, I could do this only on a level surface. When I reached the threshold of the house and tried to step over it, I could not. With surprise, almost with shame, I stared at this small wooden hurdle over which I could not raise my foot. I tried again, wobbled, and had to grab the doorjamb. Inside the house, on a bench along the wall, sat a row of old Cossack women: all straight and unflinching, with grim, unfriendly faces that were strangely dark under their white headscarves. They watched me dispassionately. Their silent hostility made me stubborn, and for the third time I tried to step over the threshold. But with this what was left of my strength vanished, and I fell on the cold clay floor. I whispered, barely audibly and plaintively, as old ladies do, mocking my own clumsiness, "Oh, my God . . ."

Mama carried me to the bench and lay me down. I did not get up again.

Even the slightest movement made me go into convulsions. My head no longer held steady on my neck; it could only lie on a pillow. Sometimes Mama would carry me out to the yard, into the sunlight, but more often I stayed in bed. Life rolled on without me. At times I would open my eyes and see everything clearly, but could neither hear nor understand what was being said around me. Other times I could not open my eyes, but could hear every little sound clearly, too clearly. On one such occasion, I heard the landlady trying to persuade Mama in the next room:

"Leksandrovna, order the three coffins at once. Simpler for you. And cheaper. She will not last two days. . . ."

"No," Mama replied. I never again heard her say no so quietly and desperately.

Before I rejoined the living, my grandmother and little sister had died.

Then the bombings started. I was already getting up. I was so used to the sound of bombs from my time in Leningrad that I wasn't at all afraid. With a strange feeling of superiority, I observed the horror and panic of our landlady and her neighbors. The train station and the railways were bombed long and hard, and we lived very close by. Huge oil tanks caught fire, and heavy clouds of thick black smoke filled the sky.

We had to leave. Father had been at the front since the first day of war, an officer and a communist. Furthermore, we had heard the Germans hated Leningraders with a passion and often shot them on sight. Mama put some things into a satchel, and off we went into the steppe. Once again we did not know where we were headed or when we would stop.

Here my memory contains some gaps. It's like an old, damaged film: some shots are clear and sharp, some have only occasional distinguishable details, and some are completely washed away by my hunger and sickness in those times. Although months had passed since we stepped off the train, I was still too weak, everything inside me was slowed down, and I could not hold on to coherent memories.

But perhaps it was simply impossible to remember such things coherently. Around me were scenes of unbridled rout and chaos. The world was flying apart into thousands of pieces. Everything was permeated by smoke and a horrible burning smell; the steppe was tight and suffocating, as if squeezed inside a hot, sooty fist. Houses burned, grain fields burned, and oil tanks burst into flame. In the disorderly retreat, some things were burned deliberately, others caught fire from the bombs. All was left to destiny's whim.

The Cossacks who lived in the area of the Kuban River were too orderly and thrifty to let anything good go to waste. They took whatever they could carry. We met a young woman along the road with two buckets of honey rocking on a yoke—taken from a collective farm, of course. An old man passed with a huge bag that kept changing shape, chickens jumping inside, squawking hysterically. At one point a storm of goose down and feathers rained down on us—someone had opened up the feather bags on a bird farm. We encountered carts, sometimes entire caravans, bursting with people's carefully covered possessions. The drivers would look at us cautiously and tensely, and whip their horses or oxen more viciously.

The sun burned terribly, but the heat seemed to come more from the fires and smoke. Sometimes the sun was nearly eclipsed by the thick black veil. And sometimes the midday darkness was pierced by the roar of German airplanes, the markings on their wings clearly visible as they passed above us. Machine guns stuttered, but whether the gunmen did not seek to hit civilians on the road or simply missed us, we remained unharmed.

Although I did not complain and did not stop, I was quickly running out of energy. It was more and more difficult to lift my feet off the ground. Every painful breath of hot air slashed my throat yet still seemed not to reach lower, down to my lungs, where it was sorely needed. I was holding Mama's hand but could not keep up with her. Every so often she would bend down, take me in her arms and carry me and I would be overtaken by an incredible joy—rest, peace, Mama's arms. I knew that her strength would not last for even fifteen minutes. But those few minutes were a paradise. I would close my eyes, not hearing the airplanes, the neighing horses, the screams. Maybe I was simply losing consciousness from weakness—but that was happiness: to stop sensing reality around me for a moment, to be liberated from the dusty road beneath my feet.

Too soon, Mama would lower me onto the grass beside the road, puffing heavily, and sit down next to me, exhausted. Even the hair on her forehead, which had escaped her scarf, was covered with gray dust.

"There's a bomb crater up ahead." She spoke with difficulty. "We'll have to bypass it through the field. Can you do it?"

"Yes," I told her. "It's okay. I can."

This was even more difficult, to step over long broken stems of wheat, which tangled around my feet, scratching and piercing them, making me stumble. The wheat was so much taller than I. Again Mama took me in her arms.

Somehow, suddenly, it all ended. Perhaps because darkness came. We managed to get far enough from the rail station, beyond the Yeia River. I don't know whether we had reached another village or simply some faraway subdivision of our Kuschevka. Here the scattered steppe settlements of a dozen or so huts were called subdivisions.

We were not let into a single hut, but it made no sense to go farther, for in the darkness we might encounter the Germans. We heard that they had already advanced far beyond us on other roads and were expected here any minute. There were poplars growing along the road, and there beneath them on the grass we settled down for the night.

Twilight was ending. Here, far from the station, the air was clean and fresh. It smelled of the steppe and of the dinner being cooked at the home closest to us, on a stove under a straw awning in the yard. People were chatting with each other there, as if nothing unusual were happening. I heard the soft, dull banging of clay dishes and bowls, which I loved. A woman was scolding someone. A dog was barking lazily—maybe because of us, maybe just to get attention before dinner.

Mama and I sat together in the dark under the poplars. The grass was soft and warm. I was very tired, but neither afraid nor hungry. I felt only the sad awareness of our homelessness, to which I had already grown accustomed. In this world, we did not have our own roof, our own door, our own dog. We did not even have our own clay bowl.

"Lenochka," Mama said. She was pulling something out of her knapsack. "You did not forget that tomorrow is your birthday?"

Only now did I see what she had put into the bag, besides food. It was easy to distinguish, even in the dark: a new white dress with flowers embroidered on it.

"You will put it on tomorrow. It's your gift. See, you will have a celebration after all."

I laid my hand on it, and this strange, forgotten feeling of new smooth fabric, of something that existed only for me, suddenly revived memories of another life. Celebration, birthday, gift . . . And there used to be a table, in our own apartment, and there had been so many of us around it, eating pies that Mama and Grandma had baked so beautifully. And now there were three graves behind us, possibly four (we had long ago lost contact with father and did not know if he was still alive), and only the dark steppe ahead of us. And somewhere in that darkness, on that very road by which we were sitting, German troops were approaching.

We hugged and kept silent. I remembered a picture from

Vadik's school atlas, left behind in Leningrad: "Notions of the earth during the Middle Ages," was printed on it. In the picture, a man has reached the edge of the earth. The earth is covered by a crystal dome, to which the sun and the moon are attached. The man is on his knees at its edge, poking his head beyond the dome and looking into the emptiness, where there are no stars, no clouds, only spinning hurricanes. So, too, were we at the edge of the earth; the edge was the road by which we sat. Beyond was a silent, menacing emptiness. And we were not the ones peeking into it; instead, it was slowly advancing upon us, having smashed through the dome shielding our earth.

After we ate something, Mama spread a soft blanket on the grass, laid me on it, and settled down beside me. Grasshoppers were chirping on the other side of the road. I lay on my back looking up at the sky. The Milky Way hung above the road. I loved walking through it with my eyes, stepping from star to star, trying to recognize what I was encountering along the way. The Small Bear? The Constellation of Hounds?

Something happened next to the Milky Way. A bright line pierced the sky, not descending like a falling star, but rising. Curves sprouted sideways from it, and fireballs lit up on the end of each curve. This was a "chandelier"—that's what we called the rockets that hung in the sky for a long time, like strands of grapes, illuminating the ground below. Then three or four of them burst into flames at once, and from far away I heard a monotonous roar. Lying there on the ground, I could feel the earth trembling.

"Mama, are those tanks?"

"Sleep and don't think of anything," she said. "Tomorrow is your birthday."

The chandeliers continued to hang over the steppe. Their deadly light seemed hostile to the Milky Way, but the Milky Way calmly remained. There was a strong smell of wormwood, and the grasshoppers were chirping louder and louder. They were joined by a chorus of frogs in the reeds by the river and these familiar sounds made the mechanical roar far away less menacing. Sleep finally came to me, and it was just as deep as if I were lying in my bed in Leningrad, back at our apartment on Lesnoy Avenue.

THE NEXT DAY Germans were everywhere, and so was danger. Though we were known in our subdivision and could be denounced by anyone, the greater danger was in wandering about in an unknown place, calling attention to ourselves. We turned around and headed back to Kuschevka.

The houses in our subdivision were subjected to mass searches. It wasn't clear why. But the villagers greeted the Germans with bread and salt. The Cossacks hated collective farming, and the Germans had dropped hundreds of leaflets from low-flying airplanes, promising a return to pre-Revolutionary land division. The Cossacks would have their land back, the way it had been for them before communism. The villagers loudly discussed these promises in front of the Leningraders, who were famous for their patriotism. Once, when Mama read a newspaper and said, "They say we shot down eight aircraft," an uneasy pause ensued. "Leksandrovna," the Cossacks asked, "whom do you call 'we'—the Soviets or the Germans?"

Only long afterward did I understand this childhood lesson, which left a bitter taste in my mouth for years to come. All of us, living side by side, were separated by barriers without entrances or exits. The lives of the Leningraders and the Cossack landladies were similarly difficult, but this was the sole thing we had in common. Our differences stood between us like a wall of alienation and incomprehension, even though our shared suffering should have bonded us together.

"Back there, on the Neva," Mama and other Leningraders would say, "we were freezing and starving to death, but nobody thought of surrender! Of course we've seen injustice and cruelty in our country! But is now the time to raise these issues, when the entire country is ablaze, in ruins, drowning in blood? Who has the right now to think about their broken life, about their confiscated field?"

"Why do you stand up for your damn Bolsheviks?" the Cossack women of Kuschevka would reply. "Look, they starved your whole city to death, and those of you who survived were thrown in railcars like cattle and driven for months so that hunger could finish you on the way. Then they dumped you here without even a piece of bread. If you want to obey such people, go ahead, but we think differently. We remember our Cossack freedom!"

In Leningrad, Mama had never heard about, and could not have imagined, the terrible famines in the Ukraine and on the Kuban steppe. How could she know? We had no relatives or friends in these places. And even if we'd had them, they wouldn't have dared write us the truth—and we'd never have received their letters, anyway. The newspapers extolled the heroism of glorious agricultural laborers, the bliss of abundant collective farming. "The people's age-old dreams have come true!"

And how could we have known the most terrible part of the truth. . . .

Mama, I am sure, learned of it later when she finally succeeded in befriending the Cossack women. But she told me nothing, I was only a child. I learned of these things many years later, as an émigré in New York. When I was no longer welcome in my own country and found myself on another continent, in another hemisphere, I began to understand much of the bitter truth about the people who had lived next to us and about the land through which we had wandered in those years.

One evening, I was skimming an article in an old issue of Roman Gul's *Novyi Zhurnal*, almost not paying attention, when the name Kuschevka jumped out at me.

The article was about a man named Vlasov, a former Red Army general who had turned against Stalin after being taken prisoner by the Germans during the war. A friend of his recounted stories from the time Vlasov served as a military commander of the Kuschevka rail station before the war. Back then,

Kuschevka was a transit stop for trains carrying farm families who had been arrested and were being sent north into exile. The man had witnessed terrible scenes that he would never forget, even during the horrors of the war. Vlasov saw his experience in Kuschevka as the turning point in his conscience.

And so it happens that an invisible finger indicates an obscure place, lost among forests or steppes, which then becomes a crossroads for immense human suffering. Thousands and thousands of people—how many could the wooden cattle cars hold, how many could the iron rails endure? First, there were trainloads of doomed women, children, and elderly, exiled from their land, their husbands and fathers and sons shot or tortured to death. Then, several years later, on these same rails, a reverse flow, from north to south, of similarly doomed, slowly dying Leningraders. Like me, unable to step over the threshold of a house.

And when I fell across that doorway, not one Cossack woman moved to help me. At that moment, they saw not me, but the exhausted, emaciated children on the trains full of exiled farmers. Farmers from neighboring villages, maybe relatives they used to visit on holidays or for weddings, who were driven north to their deaths.

North. From where the trains—maybe the same ones— were now arriving. And since we were from the north, since we were backing the north in this war, in the Cossacks' eyes we were accomplices.

How could we know?

BECOMING AWARE OF a wall between people was one of the most painful and bitter experiences of my childhood. Almost as bitter as everything else I had suffered. In Kuschevka death was not raining from the sky, nor were houses collapsing to the ground as bombers roared above. The cold did not torture me anymore, numbing my hands and feet. Hunger did not torment me with deadly emptiness, driving my entire body mad, forcing me to concentrate on one thing, only one thing: When will the next tiny scrap of bread come? The next little cup of water? No, everything was quiet. Around me life was normal, people were walking, doing chores, talking to one another, and sometimes even to us. But those people did not really exist. Not for us. There was a wall.

Perhaps the most precious gift of my destiny was that the desperation of this time forced me to focus not on the height of that wall but on the cracks in it. Look, a crack here, another there, and over there is an actual hole!

AFTER OUR UNSUCCESSFUL attempt to flee through the steppe, we returned to the house where Grandma and Tanya had died. Not long after, a tall, broad-shouldered German entered our hut, looked me and Mama up and down, and barked out an abrupt command. He pointed to our suitcase with a gesture we were used to seeing: Open it up, lay out the contents. Immediately he was tossing around our meager possessions, barely looking at them, and then he froze. He did not speak or shout, but roared deep from inside his throat. He clutched at something from the bottom of the suitcase.

He stood up and came very close. He shoved the thing in my face, then in Mama's chest. It was my father's old military shirt.

How it had gotten there, I don't know. Mama or Grandma must have packed it, hoping to exchange it for something. He kept hitting it with his fist, shouting and pointing to the officer's insignia on the collar.

His shouts were questions. He repeated the same short word. "Who?" or "Whose?" perhaps. Then: *"Offizier?"*

Mama had one supernatural quality: she was incapable of lying. She could not utter a lie; lying was a foreign language to her.

"Yes," she said. "Officer. My husband."

I don't know if the German understood. For a minute he stared at her. Mama stared back with a deadened, frozen face. She was naturally dark-skinned, and remained so even after a winter in the Blockade. But now her face had gone completely white.

They could not have stood and stared at each other like that for very long. But that minute was enough to turn one's hair gray.

Finally the German mumbled something, threw the shirt on the floor, and returned to the suitcase. He grabbed something else and stood up again. He was holding a photo of my father sent from the front; he was in full uniform, wearing his cap and Red Star. The German showed it to Mama, shouting, *"Kommunist?"*

This was easy to understand.

"Yes," Mama replied. "Communist. Officer. My husband." She spoke with difficulty, but very clearly.

The soldier grew very calm. His movements became measured and businesslike. He took the photo in his left hand, and with his right reached for the holster on his hip and removed his revolver, all the while keeping an eye on us. He pointed at me with his gun, almost brushing my face with it, and asked something else.

"Yes," Mama said. "My daughter. His daughter."

He pointed to the photo, then to me, with his gun. Mama nodded to confirm.

He also nodded, apparently satisfied. He stepped back and aimed at me. Mama came up from behind and hugged my shoulders.

I felt no fear. In our lives, death was ordinary, commonplace. And even if my conscience was clear, I was so slowed by sickness and hunger that I had no strength for fear. I stood silently, not moving. Mama, too.

For some reason he did not shoot. He lowered his hand, as if calculating. He replaced the gun in the holster but did not close it. He lifted my father's shirt from the floor and put it neatly, together with the photo, on the landlady's grand bed, next to a pyramid of pillows. Then he returned to the suitcase once more.

He threw some clothes out of it, one after another, and soon stopped again. He was scrupulously examining something else on the bottom of the suitcase. He stood, holding yet another photo, switching his eyes from it to us, and back. Something had changed inside him: his deliberation was now aggravated; he was making an intense effort to understand.

He extended the photo to Mama with a question—without hostility, just an annoyance at his inability to comprehend.

"My father," Mama said. *"Mein Vater."*

It was a pre-Revolutionary photo of my grandfather in his Orthodox priest's robe, his hair long and a heavy cross around his neck.

The German grabbed something else out of the suitcase. It was the heavy silver cross that Grandfather wore in the photograph. By what miracle had it never been exchanged for a measure of flour or butter? The crucifix lay in the German's hands, flashing at us with a dimmed but still shiny ray.

He posed yet another question, not so much to us as to himself, as he held the cross and the photo: Could it be the same one?

It was 1942, only one year since we had entered the war. This man was probably a farmer, maybe just an agricultural laborer to judge from his simplicity, which betrayed the roughness of a peasant rather than the sleekness of a drill sergeant. He had not yet hardened completely. In 1943 perhaps he would not have mulled over the cross and the photo. But in 1942 he still knew how to hesitate. A few years later, while reading *War and Peace*, I remembered this German. In one scene, Pierre is brought before Marshal Davout, and during the brief exchange of glances between the prisoner and the high-ranking officer, they became simply two fellow men.

"Das ist gut," the soldier finally said, pointing each hand— the photo, the cross—at the other. And he translated with difficulty: *"Khorosho."* Good.

He took three steps to the bed, where the shirt and father's photo lay.

"Das ist schlecht," he said, with a shade of his prior hostility. *"Plokho!"* Bad.

Then, making his final point, he laid the cross and Grandfather's photo on the bed. *"Khorosho,"* he repeated.

He stood in front of the bed, looking at all this, and shook his head, as if admitting his confusion. Then he gestured abruptly toward the suitcase—Take it away—and quickly walked out of the hut.

Mama and I stood frozen. In the corner of the living room, on the bed, lay the shirt, the cross, the two photos. We were silent.

Suddenly Mama sat down on the clay floor and covered her face with her hands. I grabbed her by the shoulders. I was scared. Death was no big deal, but I had never seen Mama lose control like this, covering her face with her palms, pressing them against her eyes with all her strength.

I NEVER MET my grandfather. He died the year I was born, in Holm, where he lived for many years and where Mama was born. Mama's godfather lived in Opochka. These were Pushkin's places. Peaceful, docile Middle Russian places. There was a cult of Pushkin in our house, and from early childhood I knew dozens of his pages by heart—"and a trip to Opochka, piano in the evening . . ." I saw photos of fields, bright birch forests, villages with dense old gardens presided over by white bell towers with their shiny thin crosses.

After the Revolution rolled through Holm, not a stone was left of the town's old life. Nor any remnant of Grandfather's old family life.

How he must have suffered I don't have to guess. Other people, who saw those like him with their own eyes, told me. I read, for example, an account by Nadezhda Mandelshtam, the writer and wife of the great Russian poet Osip Mandelshtam, in her *Memoirs:*

Somewhere in Bogoslovsky Street, not far from our home, stood a church. I remember seeing a little gathering of people there; we stopped and found out that an "expropriation" was under way. It went on very openly; I don't know if it was done so openly elsewhere. We entered the church, and nobody stopped us. An old disheveled priest was shaking, and huge tears rolled down his face as they tore down ornaments and hurled icons to the floor. Those leading the expropriation were chanting loud antireligious propaganda as old women wept and the crowd giggled, amused by this unprecedented spectacle. . . .

I don't know if the crying priest survived all this. He looked like he might have a stroke right there.

Grandfather survived, to live a bitter life of hardship. He no longer had the means to earn a living. The money he had been saving all his life, dreaming of buying a house for his family, was deposited in a bank that, like all the other banks, did not survive the Revolution. His older daughter, Talya, who had managed to graduate in time, went to work as a teacher. It was a miracle for a priest's daughter to find a job. Mama, who was still in school, was expelled. But because she was an exceptional student, she was permitted to take all her final exams immediately and thereby obtain her certificate. This required uncommon courage from the people who allowed her to do it. Mama then began giving lessons and tutoring struggling students, who sometimes were older than she. Mama's younger brother, Volodya, was still a boy. The family lived on the edge of starvation.

The new government was woefully short of people who could work in the field of education. My grandfather had been not only a priest, but also an inspector of parochial schools in his district. He was highly respected, a firm, organized, and conscientious man in everything he pursued. More important for the authorities, he knew all the schools, their peculiarities and needs, better than anyone else.

There was only one condition. Obviously, Father Alexander Luchansky would have to renounce the priesthood. There was no place for a priest in government service.

Grandfather refused.

The family lived along the road to the cemetery. From his window, Grandfather watched people being led there under guard to be shot. Sometimes they were carted, several at once. Before his eyes, under his windows, people walked the last meters and counted the last minutes of their lives.

Still, Grandfather refused.

He knew well that he would have to endure far more than the fear of jail or death. Many conversations that Mama and Aunt Talya had about those years left no doubt that he'd quickly and correctly grasped the essence of the new regime and what it would bring to the nation. Given the unbridled propaganda and violence against priests, religion, and the church—from mockery and vile curses in the newspapers, to shootings, cathedral burnings, and the destruction of icons, manuscripts, and books—he understood that, even alive and free, he was sentenced to a lifetime of loneliness, without hope or reprieve. Sooner or later, everyone would abandon him.

Ever so pervasively and perniciously, he was being isolated from people who had known him for decades, distorted by a false image, a twisted shadow: that of parasite, hypocrite, liar, a religious sweet-talker who never did anything useful and who lived at the expense of others. Long dead, he stared from his photo no more than a minute into the eyes of a German soldier, who believed him. But people who had known him for much of his life believed not him, but the lies being told about him. After the Revolution, my real grandfather lived only inside himself, and for two or three other people. To all others, he was dead. And left to walk around in his place, giggling and smirking, was an ugly shadow. It appropriated his name and, instead of taking on his life story and accomplishments, as shadows often do in tales, it blamed him for its own sins and wretchedness.

Grandfather knew this in advance. Some friends would perish without a word; others, clinging to life, would secretly ask not to be judged harshly and would hurry away from him. The most painful thing, the thing that would ravage his soul, was that there would be no family. The family obviously could not endure; his wife would, but only she. Talya was eleven during the Revolution; Galya was nine; Volodya was just an infant. They would have to grow up in a new society, under a new regime. No child's soul could endure. A child is simple, and cannot think that the entire world is wrong—that all the nice people who smile at her but avoid her father are wrong, that teachers, newspapers and books are wrong, and that only her father is right. He had planted some seeds in his children, and he could hope that at least his daughters, and perhaps his son as well, would never renounce him (and indeed they never did). But they would not believe in his righteousness despite an entire world's opposition. They would be of the world, not of him.

When Mama returned to Holm with her new husband to introduce him to her parents, my father, a young communist graduate student, considered the formal introduction sufficient and stopped speaking to his father-in-law. He had nothing to say to a class enemy, an old man who had spent a lifetime poisoning people with the opiate of religion. It was probably not a decision Father had made in advance (otherwise, a straightforward man, he would have refused to go to Holm altogether), but rather a spontaneous, uncontrollable antipathy he felt. Never, not even after Mama and Father were divorced, did Mama tell me this; I found out from Aunt Talya. Knowing Mama, I understand what feelings of shame for her husband and guilt for herself must have stood behind this lifelong silence. And what a gaping wound this remained, never to be healed.

Father's behavior was natural for those years, however. Back then, it was called "to throw overboard," "to toss into the dustbin of history." Father, firmly grounded in his beliefs, zealously accepted the rhetoric of his slogans and the practical means of their implementation—to stop talking to a persecuted old man, to break off relations with a fired coworker, to turn away from a relative who had foolishly made a politically incorrect remark in public. This was how the new world, with its incorruptible morals, was to be purified and consolidated.

Decades passed. Mama was no longer among the living. It's

good that she did not live to see my family's last, hopeless years in Leningrad. I was still working at the Hermitage Museum, and it was clear that I could remain there only at the same price that was once asked of my grandfather. With one difference: Instead of renouncing religion, I had to renounce simple decency. Aunt Talya was visiting us less and less frequently, as was everyone who knew us; but still she came. On one of her visits, the conversation turned to my troubles at the Hermitage.

"Elena should have expected all this," Aunt Talya declared. "She works at the ideological front lines."

"Can we avoid pathetic absurdities?" I asked her with fatigue. "What the hell does ideology have to do with a portrait of the Duke of Alençon, or Poussin's *Landscape with Polyphemus*, or battle paintings by van der Meulen?"

Alyosha, my husband, intervened. "Natalia Aleksandrovna, when they were persecuting your father, was that just? Was it also ideologically necessary?"

Aunt Talya had loved her father a great deal. But she did not flinch.

"He was part of an alien class."

Grandfather had known all this in advance. He prepared himself, kept his head up, and silently endured his isolation for years.

Only on the eve of his death was he delivered from his solitude. Mama sent my brother, Vadik, to her parents' house in Holm for several months. I was about to be born, and Mama could not handle two small children at once. Grandma came to

Moscow to help Mama through the birth and the first few months of her new baby's life.

This may have been the best thing I have done in my life: to be born at an opportune time. Something astonishing happened with Grandfather. A dam broke, and with desperate passion he became attached to his first grandchild—the only one he was to know. Here was an escape from the torment of loneliness. Grandfather and little Vadik would sit on the porch of the tiny house in Holm and double over with laughter, as Grandfather, in a hesitant voice, unused to speaking for so long, repeated to the boy some all-but-forgotten children's poem.

It was a happy eve of his passing. Grandfather knew that he had stood tall until the very end. That he had withstood everything. "Now, Master, you may let your servant go in peace. . . ." Vadik tightly clasped Grandfather's weakening hand with his own little one, destined never to grow big and strong.

There was nothing ahead except gratitude and immortality—for Grandfather's life was already imparted to a new one, which was only beginning.

Grandfather died that same year of a heart attack, suddenly and quietly.

It was this man who looked from an old photo into the eyes of a soldier who aimed a gun at me. What influenced the soldier? The cross, the crucifix, respect for another religion? Or something in that face, in the eyes that met his own?

One of my greatest regrets is that I was never able to visit

Grandfather's grave to thank him. For if one can save a life from the grave, why can't one say thank you through the grave? Mama and I were told that Holm was almost entirely destroyed during the war. Not even the old cemetery remains.

All that is left of that brief, happy time, when the three of them—Grandfather, Vadik, and Holm, the motherland of our family—were united, is a faded photo of my brother. On the reverse, in Grandfather's small, careful hand, is written:

Vadim Fedorovich Kozhin.
Photographed 25 September 1933
in the town of Holm.
1 year and 4 months

Vadik is standing on a chair, holding its back. His face is full of the seriousness that an especially difficult task requires, which in children often resembles a concentrated dignity. It is indeed difficult to stand on a tall chair and not move, while some strange fellow is doing something incomprehensible under a black veil, hidden behind a weird machine on three legs. But Grandfather has asked, and there he stands next to the black veil, smiling and lovingly making faces, with a special glow in his eyes. He is very happy that Vadik is standing so well and so calmly.

Behind the child, one can see a graceful, stylish white column with leaves around it—a hint of a gazebo or a terrace. To the right is an idyllic rural landscape, with a lake far below, dense treetops surrounding it, under a towering calm sky. This could have been a set decoration for Chekhov's *The Seagull*, and I recognized the lake and sky in photos that Mama's old friends later brought to her in Leningrad. They were schoolmates of hers, all astonishingly pretty, with that old-style charm of Russian provincial adolescent girls—big, truthful eyes looking straight ahead, unsmiling mouths, and perfectly parted smooth hair—in dark dresses with white collars. They sat on the shore of that same lake, beneath that same sky, as if expecting something. "I am a seagull. . . . No, not that . . ."

When I think of Holm burning during the war, I don't imagine blazing trees or houses. For some reason I always see, among the creeping tongues of flame, that fragile white column, the cardboard greenery hugging it, the peaceful lake and grove of trees lying below. A flame leaps onto the column; the lake is pierced by first a black, then a red stain. Everything shakes, as in the painful death struggle of a living being, then convulses in agony and falls into a fiery abyss.

Maybe during that very same day and hour, Mama and I were walking through the burning steppe.

I don't know what marked Grandfather's grave—a stone plaque, an iron cross, or a wooden one? Whatever it was, there is nothing left of it. There might not even be anything left of Grandfather's bones, the soil of Holm having run molten with fires, having been crushed and ground up by tank tracks, and churned by bulldozer blades. There only remains that which cannot be seen or felt, that which I most dearly want to preserve: a memory of Grandfather and his refusal to renounce his priesthood.

Maybe it will some day help someone else as it helped me. Because things repeat themselves, generation after generation. The easiest path is renunciation—of God, of oneself, of one's friends. Most people acquiesce; some do not. What helps most is to remember that there have always been people who refused. "The circumstances are stronger than you, you will have to submit," someone wrote to me once. But I knew that circumstances did not turn out to be stronger than my grandfather. That he'd endured it all to the end. I had learned that the whole world may deny a person's right to dignity, but if he has preserved it inside himself, the world cannot touch him.

I rarely thought about Grandfather's story, but it was always present inside me. Perhaps there is an invisible genetic horoscope that predetermines the fate not only of one person but of his entire lineage. It is decided not by the stars' alignment when you were born, but by words which were said (or not said) when your mother was still a girl with long black braids. Then, just as today, and a thousand years ago, an eternal choice was being made. Anouilh's Creon says: "I said yes." Antigone replies: "But I did not say yes. I can still say no to all that is repugnant to me; I want to judge it all for myself."

It is very important to know that people in your family knew how to say "no," that a link not too far down the chain was made of steel. Sometimes it is your only pillar of strength, this responsibility of being a link in that chain.

I OFTEN REMEMBERED the German's search—when we returned home to Leningrad in the fall of 1944.

In Leningrad I finally went back to school on Baburin Street. Now, after an orgy of renamings, I think it's called Smolyachkov Street. When I came home from class later than usual, I often saw columns of German POWs marching down Lesnoy Avenue from Poklonnaya Hill where they worked, taking apart ruins and putting up buildings.

Leningrad was still half-empty. There were so few people that their figures seemed to dissolve on the broad avenues. Even the monuments were nowhere in sight: They either had been taken down from their pedestals or surrounded by sandbags or wooden boards. There were many ruins, some still standing, carcasses of uninhabited houses, without roofs or floors. Cars and trolleys were rare. Squares and parks stood abandoned or partitioned for vegetable gardens. This silence, emptiness, and immobility was the city's spirit: It seemed frozen somewhere between life and death.

But every day, at the same evening hour, the same scene repeated itself. Endless columns of prisoners were led down Lesnoy Avenue. And, as if by some invisible sign, people emerged from nowhere to watch. They stood silently on the edge of the sidewalk, up close to the prisoners, unable to tear their eyes away. All these people had survived the Blockade.

Most of them were middle-aged women—but then all women, except the twenty-year-olds (and sometimes they too), seemed middle-aged. Men were nowhere to be seen, except a rare old man or a cripple from the front, and there were very few of us children.

The Germans walked by, not looking at us. Their faces were exhausted and tense. Some looked straight ahead, some walked with their heads lowered (that was most common), and a few tried speaking with each other, pretending that they were paying no attention to us.

We all stood silently. There never was a single shout, curse, or insult. Not a sign of anger or hatred. Nobody addressed them at all. We stood like a thin and immobile wall; behind us stood the ghosts of our dead. We felt something very important during those moments. Some difficult internal task was being completed, a task of silent necessity. But we could not break through to understanding what it was.

The Germans kept walking. "Stand up for the deadly struggle against the dark Fascist force, the cursed hordes." We all knew it by heart. And the deadly struggle went on, but now far away. Bombs were raining on German cities, and now it was Germans crouched in cold basements, like us two and three years ago. Now it was German children who could tell from the roar in the sky which planes were coming and what they were carrying.

But something had been displaced in us. They were no force, these prisoners, no cursed horde. Just tired, ragged, undernourished people like ourselves. Enemies and killers? Yes.

But we had no desire for revenge. So heavy was the burden, on each of us, of our yet unsuffered grief, so irreversible were our losses, so incomparable were they to anything else, that it was absurd to think of vengeance. What could we take from them, and how would it help us? Is there a vengeance that could erase my memories of Vadik's body being carried out under a blanket; of Tanya choking in her agony; of me and Mama, the last ones, trudging through smoke and thunder in a burning steppe?

We did not need vengeance. We needed something else from them. Something greater.

Some strange suppressed sound came from deep in the throat of a woman next to me. She wore an old worker's coat that reeked of engine oil. Did she want to shout out all her pain and suffering? Or was she choking back a sob at the sudden sorrow of seeing a prisoner so young: a boy without even an unshaven growth of beard, his cheeks dense with freckles? Maybe he resembled someone?

They were too similar, too much like us. This made it very hard to remember that they were the enemy. And this demanded something from us. What? We did not know. But some feeling of inescapable duty held us there on the sidewalk, watching them.

And during our silent mournful vigil, some strange flashes of light and freedom would sometimes occur—as if we were not standing there with our burdens but were slowly and laboriously ascending to some place where there is no hatred, death, homelessness, or despair. Where is this place? We did not know. But the feeling was there—that something was happening to us (and to them) during these moments, that we stood together, a half-step closer to something necessary.

They kept on walking. And the Leningrad of the early quiet autumn, the autumn of 1944, an empty and triumphant Leningrad, gazed at them and us through the bombed-out windows of condemned buildings. The clear evening sky glowed through them above us, in all its serene vastness.

AFTER THE SEARCH it became obvious that we could no longer stay near the rail station in Kuschevka. We had to leave again.

This time we found shelter in a place whose name was a bit strange: "the vegetable-garden brigade." The whole property of the former collective farm was split up into different brigades: field brigade, fruit-orchard brigade, and so on. The vegetable-garden brigade sprawled over many acres of tomatoes, potatoes, beets, sunflowers, and beans. In the middle of all these fields stood the brigade house. The house was made of clay with a straw roof, but was very elongated and resembled a barn or barracks more than a residence.

It had three rooms. The middle room was a walk-through and was the biggest, but had no stove. It had a long wooden table with benches around it where collective farmers gathered for lunch during bad or extremely hot weather. There were seeds stored here too, some packed in sacks, others simply stacked in heaps on the floor. In one corner stood rolled-up straw mats for covering greenhouses; in another, shovels and rakes were piled together. The two side rooms were smaller and had stoves; they were fit for living. Nobody had ever lived in them, but when it was cold or rainy, stablemen who lived far away would sometimes sleep there.

One of these rooms was given to an old Cossack woman, Aunt Khvenya and her little nephew Mikola. Her house had burned down during a bombing raid. The second room was given to two homeless families from Leningrad: Mama and I, and Yelizaveta Nikolayevna with her family. She had two children who for some reason had romantic Scandinavian names: her daughter Dagmara was, I think, fourteen, and her son Nirs just four.

There was a stove in the middle of the room, but a barrier towering over it divided the room in half. The back half was, of course, more comfortable—people didn't walk through it, and it was warmer. Mama immediately conceded it to Yeliza-veta Nikolayevna, explaining to me, "There are three of them, and only two of us. And Nirs is younger than you. The little one cannot be exposed to cold drafts."

Indeed, the door on our half often opened and closed. Farmers would still walk in out of habit to rest up and warm themselves by the stove, before they had to walk several kilo-meters through the autumn (then winter) steppe from one sub-division to another.

Our three families, so dissimilar, lived in peace and understanding. It was mostly Mama's doing. She calmly accepted the grumblings of Aunt Khvenya—who considered herself the privileged one, being the oldest and also a local—as well as the ineptitude of Yelizaveta Nikolayevna—a bit of a spoiled lady who could not forget the comfort of her old Leningrad life. After their frequent disagreements, Aunt Khvenya and Yeliza-veta Nikolayevna nearly always reached consensus based on Mama's quiet wisdom, and indeed often solicited her opinion.

It was also Mama's achievement that we were slowly grow-ing closer to the local people, who kept to themselves and did not trust "Commies." More and more they began conversations with us, especially with Mama. They would ask her where she used to live and work, what it was like in Leningrad when the war started. That chorus of cold sharp Cossack eyes that met me on the threshold of a hut when I fell down from exhaustion seemed long ago and far away. We were becoming accepted.

For some time they simply observed us silently. Everyone saw that Mama was always doing something: cleaning, putting things in order, washing laundry, sewing; she never turned down any work. And maybe something else attracted Cossack women to her. Mama, still a very young (she was thirty-four) and pretty woman, paid no attention to those few men who appeared in our house.

I remember well one gloomy and silent man. He wasn't a local, but nobody really knew where he was from. On the farm, he served as something of a garden inspector; for some reason he was never drafted for the war. He was tall and strong, and moved almost as reluctantly as he spoke. Even his face was silent: a firm mouth, straight eyebrows, and deeply set eyes that made his stare seem all the more fixed and harsh.

Once he rode by on his bicycle when we were in the yard. Mama had ordered two iron crosses to mark our family's graves, painted them, and was now writing names on wooden plaques. I sat near her on the grass. He greeted us, got off the bicycle, leaned on its seat, and watched Mama work. Mama kept writing; we were all silent.

"Yes, it's hard," he said suddenly. He did not speak the local dialect, but pure Russian. A long pause. "It's hard, when it's like this . . . deaths. And a person is left alone."

"I am not left alone, thank God." Mama did not raise her head. "I have a daughter. And a husband at the front."

The new pause was even longer.

"Well, all right. I guess I'll get going now . . . I've had a bit of rest here."

"Take care now," said Mama softly.

"Take care."

And he left. Soon thereafter, he stopped showing up at our place. I never heard about him again.

2|c

OUR MOVE HAD PAID OFF—we hardly ever saw Germans anymore. There was no transit road close to us, so when they would stumble across our place, they were usually lost. Or once in a while, they came looking for the sad remains of the farm's vegetable reserves. But then they would have a guide from the village with them, and we would lock our doors and stay inside. It's doubtful any German ever considered the possibility that someone might live in such a place, and none of the guides ever gave us away. Together they would ascend a hill of beets, covered with soil, and an officer would dejectedly look down—either at the (not very appetizing) beets or at the toes of his shiny boots, sullied with mud.

"That's all the beets there are," the guide would explain.

But a silent threat still hung over us. Posters were nailed up everywhere, stating that all residents must report to the German commandant's office with their passports and register. Noncompliance was punishable by death. Aunt Khvenya went immediately. Mama and Yelizaveta Nikolayevna vacillated for a long time, conferring in whispers. Finally they went too. It took a while before they came back. They had German stamps on their passports.

"The scariest thing is that they are here and we are here." Mama sounded as if she were trying to convince me and herself of something. "How can we be worse off because of this ink stain?"

She had already had a similar difficulty in the past. The words "Father: Priest" on her job applications had meant unemployment and closed doors everywhere. One of her girlfriends in an equally desperate employment situation had jumped under a train. People around her were always conniving and hiding things, but Mama continued her stubborn honesty: "Father: priest." And even when she got married, she kept her maiden name so nobody could think that she was trying to disown her father.

In fact the German ink stain made us worse off, in the end. When we finally were able to return to Leningrad and to our two-room apartment, empty and looted (the neighbor with whom Mama left keys took everything she could, from children's books to blankets and pillows), it turned out that we no longer had the right to live there. We had been dreaming so much about our walls, our windows, our own door, that these nearly uninhabitable, damp, abandoned rooms seemed like the Promised Land. We settled in, but secretly and illegally: Any day we might be evicted from there, and from Leningrad in general. Because Mama's passport was stamped by the Germans, she had been denied a Leningrad residence permit. She got bounced from one office to another, each crowded with endless queues of desperate and persecuted people, until she finally reached what everyone called The Big House—the KGB building on Liteinyi Avenue, where final decisions on all matters were rendered.

Many years later, at the university, I signed up for a seminar on St. Petersburg and Leningrad architecture, taught by Vitaliy Aleksandrovich Bogoslovsky. He looked—or actually attempted to look—like the typical mad scientist in a comedy: long lanky figure, a shiny bald skull, sudden and clumsy movements of gangly arms (that was pure play; even in his old age he remained an excellent athlete). Such defensive mimicry was commonplace then. This theatrical toolbox of tricks was so obvious that it did nothing to conceal a caustic mind. Or maybe it just failed to conceal it during these years of universal intellectual unrest, the Khruschev "thaw."

"All right, then, let's begin with Liteinyi," Professor Bogoslovsky declared, sitting down at a table and motioning for the slide show to begin. "What building shall we start with? But of course!"

And a photo of The Big House appeared on the screen.

"Well, what can one say?" the professor addressed us, measuring each and all of us with a swift and piercing look, spiced with a thorny smile. "Judge for yourselves. A telling image. Nothing to say there!"

Indeed, I never saw a photograph like it again. An unknown photographer (most likely Bogoslovsky himself) stood not facing the building, but almost next to the facade. The angle was so sharp that the bulges between windows completely swallowed the alcoves of the windows themselves. The building had no eyes or mouth, it was inhuman: blind, deaf and mute. There were only the piercing concrete vertical lines, slashing from top to bottom with a mechanical, almost maniacal, force. And we cheerful, self-confident youths ("those times will never return!") suddenly fell silent, and a chill crept across the auditorium.

Some important figure had received Mama at The Big House. She never forgot that appointment for the rest of her life.

"What's this here?" demanded the official, his deep voice

well-trained by numerous public speaking appearances. He held Mama's passport with two fingers and shook it with contempt.

Mama was silent. Rhetorical questions required no answers.

"A German commandant's stamp!" the official responded for her. "A Fascist stamp! And you, a Soviet citizen, permitted this to happen? In your Soviet passport? How? No, don't be silent! Answer me!"

Mama forced herself to speak: "Not showing up was punishable by execution."

"Oh! Execution! Afraid to die, were you?"

"I had a daughter. My daughter is the only one left. Everyone else died. Without me she . . ."

"So for you a daughter is more important than the Motherland? You sold out the Motherland!"

"To go to the commandant's office with a passport does not mean selling out the Motherland."

"Yes, it does. One must fight to the death for the Motherland!"

But of course. Just when the front was approaching Kuschevka, Supreme Commander-in-Chief's Order No. 227 thundered over the radio. "Today, July 28, 1942, Red Army troops abandoned the city of Rostov, smearing their banners with shame. . . ." Everyone was smeared with shame: the soldiers who were left lying on the streets of Rostov; those who retreated, bloodied and exhausted; and the dying Leningraders who had been sent in boxcars to the front. But shame never approached the doors of the offices where all decisions were made and all orders were signed. Shame knew its place.

It was 1944 now. Dürrenmatt had not yet written *Romulus the Great:* "When a country starts killing people, she always calls herself the Motherland."—"But don't we have to love the Motherland above all else in the world?"—"No, my daughter. Above all else, we must love humans. . . ."

"And now you want to reside in Leningrad! The city of heroes!" the official was entering a phase of profound ecstasy, inspired by the beauty of his own monologue and the defenselessness of his audience.

"Because I came from Leningrad, I was put on the list of people to be shot. Both my daughter and I. If our army had come a month later . . ."

"You dare talk about our army! Those like you were not even worth saving!"

"Why shouldn't I talk about the army? My husband has been at the front from the first day of war. Every one of our families had somebody at the front. Why shouldn't the army save us?"

The official was taken aback for a moment.

"Don't hide behind your husband! He's at the front, but you—there it is, the German stamp—you were in occupied territory!"

"Is it my fault that we, the dying ones, were driven straight into the occupation?"

Eventually, only because of my father at the front, we were permitted to stay in Leningrad. But Mama was forbidden from ever working as a teacher again. People who had lived in occupied territory forever lost their access to many careers—"educating the rising new generations" chief among them. What could children learn from a woman who had a German stamp in her passport?

Two years ago a German had entered our hut during a search. We were enemies. We were from Leningrad, which stood for all that Germans hated. We were the family of an officer, who somewhere at the front was shooting at this man's friends and who someday might shoot at him too. But it took so little, really, for something human in him to rear its head. What did he find out about us that was so special? That we were saving a cross and a photo of an old priest?

Yet there was Mama, in The Big House before an important figure. He and she were part of the same nation, on the same side in this war. He knew much about Mama that could stir something human inside him. Before him stood a tormented, sick, badly dressed woman who had aged before her time. She had survived the hunger of the Blockade; buried almost all of her family; lived in the occupied territory under constant fear of death; and had not seen for years (didn't know if she'd ever see again) her officer husband. She was only asking that she and her last remaining daughter be permitted to live in their own two rooms—deserted rooms that nobody needed in an empty city.

Yet nothing human stirred inside the official. He and Mama were not on the same side after all. They were not part of the same nation. This wall had no cracks.

"ARE THEY REALLY people?" Mama had once asked. Not about the official at The Big House, but in response to something that happened when we were first in Kuschevka.

The front was quickly approaching. Grandma was already dying or had just died. It became obvious that Tanya was dying too. Her agony was excruciating: she was choking and wheezing. It may have been diphtheria or angina. The pain in her throat made her unable to swallow anything, or say anything, and she had even nearly stopped moaning. Mama lost her head and rushed into the village in the crazy hope that she would find a doctor and bring him to her little girl. She ran there, on a road ripped apart by bomb craters, under the thunder and machine-gun bursts of airplanes that streaked above the burning steppe. She sidestepped cars and carts, barely avoiding falling under their wheels.

In the village, she encountered the wild chaos of a panic-stricken retreat. All office doors were either bolted shut or, instead, swung wide open. Right beneath their windows, bonfires of abandoned archives were burning. The wind was blowing shreds of charred paper down the streets and out into the steppe. Here and there lay chairs, drawers for card catalogues, lace-bound accounting books, broken or ripped apart. But the houses that stood out with their solid privileged opulence—the houses of party bosses—were surrounded by automobiles and carts. Servants were fidgeting and running around outside, obeying orders barked out from open windows:

"No, not there! Put it under the suitcase! Did you pack away my chandelier? The chandelier!"

People carried furniture from these houses, huge bags of linen or clothing, heavy boxes. One car—Mama was stunned by this above all—was being loaded with pillows and feather beds.

"Feather beds," she said in disbelief. "They thought about feather beds . . . are they really people?"

Mama darted among fires, cars, and furiously neighing horses whose hair caught those flying shreds of burning paper. "Doctor! Where's a doctor? Where's the hospital?" The hospital was empty, of course, and there was no doctor anywhere. Suffocating from the smoke, Mama half ran; half walked back: Three dying people waited for her at the hut.

I was sitting outside in my dulled, nearly mute state, when Mama came running in the gate, already wobbly on her feet. One look at me—okay, she is still alive—and she, trying to utter something but unable to do it with her scorched throat, rushed inside the house. I heard a scream. It was such a scream . . . even I perked up, and weakly screamed something in reply. I tried to get up—but could not.

Mama ran out into the yard with Tanya in her arms. My little sister's head was lolling on Mama's shoulder, her eyes already closed. Only her tiny mouth was still moving, trying to open, gasping for air.

"My little bird! My little bird, don't fly away!"

And with her last remaining strength, Mama was raising Tanya's tiny body up, up to the blackened sky, full of smoke and thunder, as if there she might breathe easier.

"My little bird!"

But my little sister was already dead.

I COULD NEVER FORGET this, of course. But I don't know how much more life is ahead of me, and I have come to believe that it would be a betrayal to allow all this to perish with me—all that I alone saw, and continue seeing so many years later. Mama's desperate scream, heard by nobody except a half-living me amidst the thunder and wailing, as she raises up my little sister's already lifeless body. The cup of desperation and sorrow that was given to our family reached its high-water mark in that moment, and we were already drowning in it. Mama and I were left alone, face-to-face with death. And death was advancing on us from everywhere. It was swooping down from the sky, pacing next to us on the road, and taking root inside our own emaciated, helpless bodies.

These moments are like a fixed, burned-in line across my heart. Only a thread was separating what a human can endure from what she can no longer withstand. And Mama managed to endure, and to drag me by the hand out of the blackness, becoming a measure for me of what a human can and must do when everything is against her. That measure invariably stood up, later on, next to anything else that would happen in my life. And each time it was clear to me: No, it's far from being that bad. I can still hold on. I must persevere.

AT THE GERMAN COMMANDANT'S office in the main village of Kuschevka, far from the vegetable garden brigade, they asked Mama and Yelizaveta Nikolayevna about their children's ages: "They must go to school. There will be a German school in the village."

"Hitler's school," Mama said when she returned. "Never."

I had already recovered somewhat from my weakness and my sickly apathy for everything around me. Something like a tiny spark of happy resistance flashed in me. I wanted to go to school. When Vadik, one and a half years older than I, went to first grade, I had envied him terribly. Secretly, I would peek into his schoolbooks, into his notebooks, where he wrote with his amazingly steady and level handwriting: "Mama went to the garden." No toys inspired in me as much admiration as his schoolbag and his pencil case. I was so eagerly awaiting the autumn of 1941, when I was supposed to enter school.

But by the autumn of 1941, there was not a single school

left near us. Some were bombed, others converted into hospitals. And that amazing life, where kids sit in front of an imposing blackboard with white letters, where maps with ornamental hemisphere disks hang along walls like huge rugs, where the teacher's pointer floats along blue oceans, became unreal. Just as unreal as that life where people gather around a table, electricity lighting a bright lamp above, and plates full of food before them, where you can ask for seconds between the talk and laughter . . .

"So I won't study at all." I didn't even ask this, I just said it quietly.

"No, you will. I will teach you myself," Mother said. "You, and Dagmara, and Mikola, and Nirs—everyone who won't go to their school."

"How can you do it?"

"I am a teacher, remember."

"And it will be like in a school?"

"Just like in a real school."

Mama kept her word. Lessons started in the autumn. Indeed, Mama had been a teacher of Russian language and literature. But it seems she never got to work in a school where one teacher teaches history, another arithmetic, and a third Russian. Such schools never had jobs for her. ("Social origin: father—priest . . .") Her schools were only one room, in a hut or an old garrison, and she had to teach every subject. She would get assignments only in some godforsaken neck of the woods, Zhelonka village in the Novgorod region, or something on the other edge of the country, in Kzyl-Orda, where nobody wanted to go work. Her schools were full of older teenage boys who were about to be drafted and were already in their combat boots and army jackets. With obedience and confusion they stared at a young girl with braids curled up around her ears, who paced between them with a grammar book in her hands.

She used to tell me about going to Kzyl-Orda. One of her friends worked there, and during an especially difficult period Mama got a letter from her. She was inviting Mama to come and live there. She insisted that there, on the edge of the country, far from the metropolis, government agencies, and inspectors, life was more calm and free. That there were plenty of jobs since people were reluctant to come to such faraway places, and that nobody would give a damn about the "questionable" parts on her application. Mama thought for a while, wrote her friend that she would come, packed some things and bought a train ticket.

But when she arrived in Kzyl-Orda, her friend was no longer there. Either she did not get Mama's letter, or Mama did not get her reply. Mama had spent all her money on the trip, and she had no job. There wasn't even anyone to consult with—few people spoke Russian there. So Mama walked back to the rail station, the only place in town she knew, and sat down on a bench.

Kzyl-Orda was a ragged place, abandoned and sparsely populated, with tiny low huts. Its "streets" were dirt roads with sand and sickly grass on the side. But on one of them, far away in a cloud of dust, something strange was emerging. Down the road trudged a sad donkey, and riding it was an equally sad, old Kazakh man wearing a robe and a skullcap. Neither seemed to know or care where they were headed.

"I looked at him," Mama told me, "and for some reason thought that he maybe had a mean, bossy wife who had really given him a hard time. He was so downtrodden, yet so endearing—his head was bowed, so was the donkey's; his feet were dragging in the dust, and so were the donkey's hooves. I don't know why I enjoyed them so much, but for some reason I felt so funny and light! I looked at them, and said to myself: Why am I feeling so low? So what if I have no job and no money? I'll find both! I am young and strong, and I want to work. Since I am here, that's where I'll stay, and everything will be okay!"

She followed this pair with her eyes, until they disappeared, And then she got up and went back into town. Her years in Kzyl-Orda turned out to be one of the brightest chapters of her youth.

Mama told me this story frequently. Once I asked: "And what if the old man didn't pass by?"

"Well . . . I don't know," Mama answered.

But the expression that flashed across her face made me understand that if the old man hadn't passed by, something else would have happened. Everything inside Mama was already geared up for stubborn resistance, for a challenge to her own misfortune and unhappy circumstances. Somebody was destined to pass by. Something was destined to happen.

AND SO, despite everything, we began to study. It was as if all those poor provincial schools, where Mama had spent her youth working, now provided her a reliable foundation. Where a professional teacher from an excellent school would have thrown up her hands in despair, Mama operated with an habitual ingenuity, finding a way out of every dead end. Somewhere she found schoolbooks. She taught history and geography herself, from memory. As for arithmetic, everyone had different assignments: Little Nirs was counting with an abacus; Mikola and I were required to learn the multiplication tables by heart; and Dagmara was very advanced, far ahead of Mikola and me. But I was content so long as I could sit at this clean table with a book in the middle of it and learn about subjects and predicates, about the Ural Mountains that separate Europe and Asia, and proudly notice how Yelizaveta Nikolayevna and Aunt Khvenya spoke at half-volume to avoid bothering us.

There was only one problem, which even Mama could do almost nothing to fix: We had nothing to write with and nothing to write on. Even when a clean notebook showed up at the flea market, it cost an astonishing amount of money. We couldn't afford such luxury—even the locals could only buy single sheets to write letters to the front. And since the Germans' arrival, all connections with the front had been cut off, so paper had simply disappeared. As if the Chinese had not yet invented it. We used up the margins of old newspapers and wall calendars, but there weren't too many around. More often, as long as the weather permitted, we wrote with sticks on sand. We almost never saw ink or pens. And even when they appeared by some miracle, they were saved for letters. Because someday the Germans would leave (we all believed in victory, collectively and unswervingly), and we would start writing to the front again, to Leningrad, and everywhere.

These childhood years without ink and paper left their mark. I never learned to hold a pen or pencil correctly. When I returned to Leningrad and entered third grade, everyone was already writing easily and quickly and the teacher, with a class of more than forty girls, had no time to train me. Even today, when I write something in front of strangers, I occasionally catch someone's gaze fixed on my hand and the odd way that I hold my pen.

But still, it was school! We always had something to solve, to learn, to remember by heart. In our lives, full of danger and uncertainty, a seemingly stable and safe tiny island appeared, where everything was clear and measured.

"But this is very risky, isn't it?" Yelizaveta Nikolayevna once said to Mama quietly. "The fact that they don't go to the German school can still be explained. It's far, roads are in disrepair, it's cold and they have no shoes or coats. But the fact that you are teaching them . . . because it was declared: only with their permission, only under their curriculum . . . aren't you afraid?"

"Children must learn. As it is, they have had no child-hood."

"Of course not. But what can you do?"

"You can always do something."

Mama often repeated this phrase. She always said it in a simple, matter-of-fact manner, and the "something" always seemed somehow natural and obvious.

I remembered it many years later, when I was working at the Hermitage. Whenever there was word of plagiarism or some other manipulation on the part of the museum administration, my colleagues had a habit of saying, "What can we do?"

They would sigh, with a tired shrug of their shoulders—shoulders clothed in fashionable suits brought home from business trips overseas. These women knew how to succeed. Their manners betrayed them as women who eagerly obeyed their masters, who might in turn give them something: permission to publish an article, make a speech at a prestigious conference, or take another trip abroad.

Hearing that phrase, seeing those shrugging shoulders, I remembered Kuschevka. And I thought, perhaps, that I had found a simple scale for the measure of human dignity, or strength of human spirit: Does a person say, "What can we do" or "You can always do something"? Then I thought how lucky I was that, in our sorry little hut in the middle of a steppe, I had so often heard someone say: "One can always do something."

AUTUMN AND WINTER were hard for all of us. Aunt Khvenya, who had preserved some personal property, was able to get by. As for me and Mama, we had gotten a brief reprieve right before the Germans arrived, having located father, via correspondence. This had entitled us to an "attestation," a modest subsistence for families of combat personnel, which meant at least some money. But with the occupation, this obviously ended. Mama continued bartering the remains of our possessions for food. Cossack women would visit us, examining Mama's last suit—English-style, dark navy blue. They would feel it from all sides, checking the quality of the fabric, the durability of the seams, the folds—was anything worn out? They bartered tersely and even unwillingly. It was a tormenting experience for Mama, who was embarrassed, blushing, and even stuttering. It burned her lips to ask for a little more money. And probably to this day, at the bottom of some heavy trunk in that village, lies grandfather's silver cross. The same one, from the photo. It may have saved us twice.

Life in the vegetable-garden brigade itself had some lifesaving benefits. Even though the Germans had proclaimed in their leaflets that they would abolish collective farming immediately, land was not redivided. Throughout the seven-month occupation an ambiguous situation persisted. The old owners were gone, but there were no new ones either. It was impossible to understand whose land it was now, and how one was sup-posed to work on it.

So the same two horses, Spunky and Red, remained in the collective stable. Hay remained in the barn, and seeds were still piled in our main room. Collective farm women who visited us began openly discussing how we would be idiots if we didn't start taking the unclaimed vegetables which were also around. So we had potatoes, beets, and a little cabbage and corn. Aunt Khvenya brought her cow to the stable. And since Mama washed and milked her, and I helped take her to pasture when I got stronger, we started getting some milk too. Our remain-ing things were bartered in exchange for flour, sunflower oil, and pig lard. Our diet, though meager and insufficient, was nothing like it had been under the Blockade, so we handled the habitual feeling of undernourishment without difficulty.

It was much harder to contend with the draining feeling of constant danger. I was regaining strength, and gone now was the numbness that had shielded me from worry. I was beginning to notice how Mama's and Yelizaveta Nikolayevna's faces changed, how they fell silent when some noise came from the road, or some unknown voice was heard from the yard. I would catch shreds of their conversations—spoken at half-volume so the children wouldn't hear. *Someone was arrested in the village again . . . they say three of our paratroopers were captured in the steppe, . . . they were shot, of course. . . . is it really true that so-and-so also became a police col-laborator? . . . Is it true that the commandant's office is preparing a list of people to be shot? . . . Leningraders?* Then I could not hear anymore. What about Leningraders?

For the first time in my life I was experiencing the especially bitter taste of grief suffered in solitude. None of the people who visited the brigade were hostile toward us—their lives were hard too, but their concerns had nothing in common with ours. Even things that could have united us—a husband, a son, a father at the front—were off-limits. We were aliens. If soldiers took us away to the commandant's office, these people would have shaken their scarf-wrapped heads in sorrow for a moment, then simply turned away from the road.

This was very hard for me to get used to, the first crack in my notion of human relations. My nine-year-old conscience had presumed that people would stick together and help each other. Nobody taught me this, but I had seen it every day. That's how it was in our family—three children and two women in blockaded Leningrad. That's how it was in the bomb shelter underneath our apartment building where residents would sometimes descend, despite the typical Leningrader's arrogant disdain of danger, when shells began exploding too close to home. Every family had blankets and even mattresses there, in their permanent little corners, a small supply of the most necessary things. But someone immediately would ask a neighbor for a smoke, another would offer a cup of hot water from her teapot: it was a ritual which immediately switched on the currents of communication. In that low-ceilinged basement lit by two or three flickering broiler lamps (tiny bottles or flasks of kerosene, each covered by a metal lid in the middle of which, through a drilled hole, stood a metal tube with a wick), faces were almost invisible. We recognized each other by voice. Everyone spoke slowly and quietly: Everyone was very weak. The voices were like the tiny flames of the broiler lamps. But every person there needed somebody else, and last drops of precious energy were spent on this conversation which stretched out like a thin thread.

One fall day, during the Blockade, we were visited by Aunt Talya, Mama's older sister. She lived alone on the other side of Leningrad, near the Obvodnyi Canal. We rarely saw her after the city's public transportation system stopped functioning. Furthermore, as a young single woman she was drafted to dig trenches in the suburbs. Digging was very hard work, but was rewarded with a bonus food ration; and there was already nothing left to eat in the city. I don't know how Aunt Talya reached our Vyborg-Side neighborhood, across the Neva River, perhaps by foot. But she felt compelled to come, bringing us almost the entirety of her bonus bread ration.

This was impossible and incredible: There were two loaves of bread on our table. When was the last time we saw so much? I jumped to my feet and ran down the stairs like I had not run for a long time. I had to find Vadik, who'd gone out for a walk. Our favorite places for a stroll had dwindled to a few—the ones closest to us, so we had enough energy to reach them— and it was easy to find Vadik. I caught up with him near the Nobel Houses, under the big granite arch.

"Hey, Vadik, you know what? Want some bread?"

My brother turned to me, and I still remember the expression on his handsome face, which was not just thin but already emaciated and bloodlessly pale. Slowly incomprehension gave way to disbelief, and then finally, as I chokingly explained everything, to shining stunned happiness. We grabbed each other's hands and ran home, laughing, just like before the war, as I kept hurriedly telling the story: "And she brought it all for us! It was a package this big, first wrapped in a tablecloth, then in newspaper, then in a bag . . . "

I remember well that in all our happiness, neither Vadik nor I were surprised by what Aunt Talya had done. The stunning event was having *two* loaves of bread on the table; the fact that she shared them with us seemed natural. Anyone in our family would have done the same. One Blockade winter, when a completely fantastic event occurred—an unknown woman on the street tipped me with a chocolate candy for helping her with some small task—I brought it home and cut it into five pieces. We were one family. And even when our neighbor and friend, Maria Aleksandrovna, got a bottle of cottonseed oil somewhere, she brought some over to us, to share.

During the very first months of war, Mama and Grandma had an argument. Its outcome determined, with simplicity and finality, how we would live. They rarely argued at all, and never for so long. This one, however, lasted for days. Neither one would give in. They would stop talking to each other, then in an hour or two flare up again. We could not avoid hearing it, and Mama and Grandma (this was uncommon too) made no effort to hide anything from the children. I think Mama wanted us to understand.

An early evacuation of the families of military personnel had begun in Leningrad. I believe it was limited to families of

officers only—I remember Mama and Grandma remarking
sadly, "How unfair." People were put into airplanes, and within
hours they would land somewhere in the fertile South or in the
Altai Mountains, which the Germans never reached. Anyone
who could rushed across this life-saving bridge in a heartbeat.
Leningrad's stores were already empty, the Badayevskiye Warehouses (which were full of food) burned down suspiciously in
the first days of the siege, and the famine was already beginning. Streets were being shelled, bombing raids were becoming
increasingly frequent, and houses burned in every neighborhood.

Mama went to the bureau which administered the evacuation. Her documents were checked, and she was offered seats
on an airplane departing in a few days. With one condition: no
seat for Grandma.

"We are evacuating members of the military man's immediate family. Wife and children must be evacuated. Mother-in-
law is not covered. She is your mother, not his. We have orders.
Miss, don't delay everyone. No. We have no authorization. I am
booking you and your three children. Stop talking nonsense.
What do you mean you are canceling the reservations?"

Mama said that we would not fly like this. Either everybody or nobody. She turned down the reservations and left the
bureau. Grandma demanded that Mama return and agree to fly
without her.

"You are a mother and are responsible for your children,"
Grandma argued, firmly and incessantly. "Children must be
saved above all else. What will you say to Fedya if even one of

them dies from hunger or bombings? You will have no excuse that nothing could be done. Or that you misunderstood the danger. Everyone knows the warehouses have burned down, and we cannot even hope for a postponement of famine. And this famine will be terrible, worse than the Civil War. The chances of breaking through the Blockade are nil—we all hear the news from the front. The children must be saved. I have lived my life, and it was a long one—sixty years. If I stay here alone, I will be dying calm and happy, knowing that you all are alive and have been rescued. And why is it certain that I will die, anyway? People die in good times and survive in hopeless times, God figures that out. All that matters is that my soul feel at peace. That will not happen if I know that I'm a burden to the family, that three children were left in danger because of me. For me, for my own peace of mind, please do it!"

I never heard Grandma talk so much, either before or since. But now she was doing virtually all the talking. Mama replied rarely, sparsely, and with difficulty.

"No. We will survive together or die together, but we will not separate," Mama said. "I assume all responsibility. Before the children and Fedya. If the children are destined to survive, they will not be thinking that they survived at someone's expense, that someone was left to die alone. It's not just lives we are saving. No. Everybody or nobody."

I did not realize that for the first time I was seeing people at a crossroads where there was no easy answer—even without an ominous sign on a white stone like in Russian childhood tales. In such circumstances, everything is tied together in a tormenting knot. It cannot be untied, only slashed with the blade of internal commandments, which are embedded in the very nature of a person's soul. Mama was deciding not which option was better, but which option was in one way or another impossible.

Among us children, the first mention of evacuation caused unbridled celebration. The adventure of a trip on an airplane, and then beautiful places—fields and forests, a sky without bombers, an unlimited supply of bread! But when Mama returned from the bureau, everything in our minds became confused. Without Grandma? All children love their grandmothers, but we loved our Grandma in a very special way. She lived with us, and it was from her, as much as from Mama, that the rivers of our prewar happiness flowed. Mountains of smiling pies; islands of cream puffs floating in golden, milky vanilla sauce; little aprons, shirts, and dresses embroidered with funny faces and creatures, with strands of berries or flowers; fantastic New Year's decorations that she helped us glue together from multicolored paper and foil; long ribbons, stars, booklets, firecrackers, or tiny bags in which surprise gifts were hidden. When we coughed or complained of a sore throat, Grandma was the first to cure us, and all of her remedies were aromatic and tasty. A tiny piece of sugar was melted in a silver spoon next to a burning candle; Danish King's drops dripped and dissolved in a transparent glass. This miraculous and cozy home alchemy made even the flu seem harmless.

But Grandma was also the main arbiter of justice in our home. Even Mama could sometimes get it wrong—who was truly guilty of the prank?—punishing Vadik instead of me or vice versa. Grandma never got it wrong though. Perhaps some sign in our faces let her figure out who was shoving whom under the table until both spilled soup. Or perhaps it was some supernaturally sensitive observation, some knowledge of all of us by heart. Not willing to be severe (maybe she thought that our father fulfilled more than all three adults' allotment of severity?), she was always fair. Her justice, which levied no punishment but only condemnation, knew no favorites or exceptions.

Once I accidentally overheard Grandma chastising Mama in another room. Hunger had begun, and every scrap of bread or spoonful of food was followed with worried glances around the table. But I did not notice that Mama had let Tanya lick up the remains of flour or kasha from a pan in the kitchen. Grandma did notice.

"Everything must be split evenly among the children. For them this is essential—to have faith in our constant fairness, especially yours. If they start to doubt you, that will be the worst. And you, today, with that pan . . ."

"Mama, she is the smallest one, the weakest one." My mother spoke in a weary whisper. "You can see how she has become pale over the last month, lethargic and apathetic . . . And there was so little—well, maybe two spoons . . . How could I have split that up for three? Next time I'll give it to one of the others."

"Galya, Galochka, you cannot delay fairness until next time. They must believe that every time, every minute you are fair to all of them equally. Yes, even two spoons should have been split up for three. Life will only get uglier later. And only one thing will sustain them—their unswerving faith in you, me, and each other. May God save you from depriving them of that faith."

"Mama, I cannot get used to it . . . how they stare at food nowadays. Tanya just walked into the kitchen and stared at the empty pan . . . I couldn't resist."

"I understand. To get used to it . . . it's impossible to get used to it. But you must always remember that there are three of them. Everything must be equally shared, with no exceptions. A spoon of food, a spoon of fairness—that's how it is measured nowadays. Please, Galya, my dear . . ."

I heard Mama sobbing quietly.

To abandon Grandma alone?

We were just children. Quite possibly, our initial shock—without Grandma?—could have been easily subdued, converted into "nothing can be done" acceptance. They could have explained to us that Grandma herself doesn't want to go (which was true); that many families are forced to separate like this (wasn't that true?); and that we would certainly try to have Grandma join us later, by train (which could become true). But Mama, with her directness, forever drew a merciless line between truth and half-truth for us. All things were called by their proper names. And so none of Grandma's sincere, passionate, and argumentative eloquence resonated with us at all. We only heeded Mama's simple repetitive, "Everybody together or nobody." Without Grandma—never.

After several days, when Grandma finally gave in (all dead-lines had been missed by then anyway) and Mama won, it was also our victory. We were all staying together.

Never, never did Mama tell the story about that first evac-uation. She never spoke of it. Once, when I was an adult, I asked her about it, perplexed by my own potentially incorrect recollection. No, it was all correct. But even after so many years, Mama did not want to, and probably could not, talk about it. Only then did I understand what a burden she carried in her soul all those years. "I assume all responsibility." All those years, for the rest of her life.

Mama was a softer, shyer person than most. And only at some rough, merciless junctures in her fate did some stubborn unyielding power break through in her—something from her father, who was incapable of renunciation. From somewhere in-side came her absolute knowledge, despite all else, of what she must do.

An acquaintance of ours, Lebedev, one of father's cowork-ers, was arrested in 1937, and a few months later his wife, Anna Iosifovna, was arrested too. Mama took their daughter, who was left all alone, into our family. She lived with us until her uncle, to whom Mama had written, arrived to pick her up. (We later found out that he turned his niece over to an or-phanage.) I don't know if Mama was aware that she was break-ing the law that stated that Soviet citizens were forbidden from helping the "enemies of the people."

This girl, a little older than I, was an "MFEP"—a Mem-ber of the Family of Enemies of the People. We all knew that lesser acts got people arrested. And this wouldn't have even been renunciation—to simply look the other way, to avoid thinking about the fact that somewhere in a looted apartment sits a hungry, abandoned little girl. "She has her own relatives"; "We can't risk the lives of our own children for somebody else's"; "You can't help everyone"—there were plenty of half-truths which invited escape via a bypassing route. But perhaps that's really the only reason we survived—because Mama did not know or want to know such half-truths. Because she knew something else.

THE DEEPER WE GOT into autumn, the tighter grew the circle of dreariness that closed around our hut. Perhaps the poet Ivan Bunin was right: "Russian man, like the caveman, is subject to the whim of nature." But probably any person is more apt to submit to feelings of despair in the furious pounding of cold wind than on a gorgeous summer day. We were ever aware that if the already cracked window glass broke there would be nothing to replace it with. If the dried-up old door could not be fixed, then our hut would be overtaken by the cold overnight, once the frosts arrived. If tomorrow the pouring rain did not subside, then the last firewood would run out and, even if we ventured out into the steppe, we could only bring back soaked bunches of tumbleweeds and branches.

But our house had a motto: "You can always do something."

Better than the rest of us, Mama knew that our main problem was not the cold, the poverty, or even the very real danger. Rather, it was that universal hopeless gloom which had firmly settled inside our hut and was increasing its dominion over each of us. On one particularly dreary day, she quietly dressed up warmly, took a big bag, and went off to the village.

I don't know how or when she had the time to meet and befriend all kinds of different people there. They included an old man and wife, retired teachers. I think their family name was Churakov. I never once saw these people, who did so much for us. Trips to the village were both long and dangerous, and I had not yet fully recovered my strength.

The Churakovs had a big library, which they had been compiling their whole lives. Without hesitation they offered Mama full access to this sole treasure of theirs, easily and naturally, as only truly generous people do. They never thought about the risk to the books—they did not think in such terms. Mama knew instinctively how to find people like them everywhere. She returned to the house with a big, tightly packed bag: fairy tales for Nirs; Stevenson, Jack London, and James Fenimore Cooper for me and Dagmara; nineteenth-century Russian novels for the adults. And that evening we were not bothered by the cold, the rain, or noises from the road.

In Leningrad we had left behind a great children's library, which I virtually knew by heart. Masses of poetry from Zhukovski to Chukovsky, tales by Perrault, Andersen, Hoffmann, Hauff, and the Brothers Grimm, *The Thousand and One Nights*, my favorite Mark Twain, Jules Verne, Myne Reed, Boris Zhitkov adventure stories, books about animals and birds, plants and rocks, children's editions of Tolstoy and Cervantes, Kuprin and Garin-Mikhailovsky, Swift, Gogol, and Aksakov. But the amazing hours I had spent with them were firmly planted in my incredible prior life, which I now remembered as a fairy tale, not as something real. It was impossible to imagine that it could happen again, here in the steppe. And now something shook inside me, when, despite the Blockade, the rail journey, the fires, and the steppe storms, Dick from Robert Louis Stevenson's *Black Arrow* once again repeated in the king's face: "Mine be the loss!"

How much had transpired in the two years since I had heard those words! They now sounded not with the previous negligent challenge, they smelled of bitterness—for Dick now knew much about life and its losses, but his knowledge was better and more enlightened than the king's, and he knew well how to reflect his contempt: "Mine be the loss!"

We ceased living on an island that day. I felt the emptiness around us filling up again—with new people, or old ones I was recognizing anew after a long separation. Reading my old favorites was especially exhilarating. My old friends seemed to have changed just as much as I had, though they still felt close and familiar. And, most importantly, they linked me with my past. If there had been a past, then there might also be a future. And if so, then today, which was so gloomy and unreliable, was far from being the last day of our lives. Suddenly life was enlarged, and for the first time in many months hope glimmered ahead.

Everybody rushed to read the books. During the day there were plenty of household chores to do, so we read in the evenings. That's when we noticed with surprise that evenings could be a special, beautiful time. From dawn to dusk every minute was fraught with danger. But in the evenings, we were shielded by that which before had tormented us the most—isolation, cold, rain, wind, and darkness. It was indeed difficult to imagine that any German or police collaborator would embark on a journey to arrest us in the pouring rain or blowing snow. So the arrival of evening came to mean safety, a postponement of danger for many hours, until next morning—forever!

This realization turned our whole life upside-down. Gone was that subdued grief which descended upon the house with the first signs of twilight, when we could only look forward to sitting in a half-dark room, rain outside the window, the hysterical squeaking of an old awning in the yard; when the adults and Dagmara were incessantly fixing or sewing something; when we, the younger ones, wandered aimlessly around dark corners and bickered with each other out of boredom. Never before or since have I seen books fill and enlighten life so much. We no longer felt lonely; the topics for conversation were endless.

And we children talked not about books but about people, just as real as ourselves. Melissa Smith, Bret Harte's "M'liss," was for me not a literary character but a close friend. Knowing the story almost by heart, I still picked up the book again and

again, to visit M'liss. I loved her resistance and defiant deci-
siveness.

As for the boy characters, Huckleberry Finn soon outdis-
tanced the rest. His adventures were no games. He and Jim
were alone on that raft, just two of them—nobody to fall back
on. They floated down a beautiful and immortal river. But its
shores were inhabited by strangers. As I read, I was tossed from
the funny to the merciless, from ecstasy to despair. Some people cheated and killed each other, others were ready to give a
stranger their last piece of bread. Something here resembled our
own lives. What's the difference between the Mississippi and
the Neva, or the Yeia, which flowed not far from our hut? Nobody knew what awaited them beyond the river's next bend.
People were being killed all around us, and any one of us could
be killed any day. And every morning began the same way:
What will we eat today? What will keep the stove lit? How will
we survive until sunset?

In the morning we would hear the noise of a car from the
road. We would bolt the door from the inside, and Yelizaveta
Nikolayevna would whisper to Nirs to go to the corner and be
silent. Dagmara and I did not need to be told. The window
could be covered by a straw mat prepared ahead of time. Just
in time. Surrounded by two police collaborators, a German
officer walked across the yard. We watched through a crack,
standing frozen next to the window, as they crossed the yard to
the vegetable piles already covered by snow. They disappeared
behind the barn, and nothing could be seen or heard anymore.
For a long while. Terribly long. Then again: across the yard

past the vegetables piles, back toward the road. He didn't even look our way. We didn't move. They might still . . . We heard a car engine and immediately turned our heads that way, but nobody said a word. The engine stopped. We stopped breathing, the silence piercing our ears and squeezing our throats. A shout in German. Again silence. Then an engine! And then we could hear the sound moving. Away! Further away . . . and finally no longer audible.

A reprieve. It passed us by. Yelizaveta Nikolayevna would sit down on the bench and sob, "This is torture . . . one more day . . . I will not be able to endure . . ." But we all knew that we would endure. We had been spared for another day, or maybe two—given such amazing luck, how could we not endure?

So our raft kept floating across the beautiful white steppe, and a holiday shone—another day of life bestowed upon us. There, up ahead, under an evening kerosene lamp, I could already see the stars above the Mississippi.

Soon there was another change in our house. Mama and Yelizaveta Nikolayevna had been complaining to each other that we children had gotten too used to the local dialect. It was similar to the Ukrainian language, and we had begun to speak it regularly, even within the family. Mama, accustomed to the pure Russian of Pushkin, would be horrified when she heard me stress the wrong vowel. "What did you say? Partially? Where did you hear that?"

Once after I committed a particularly grave pronunciation crime, Mama declared that it was time to put an end to this. She proposed daily sessions of reading aloud. We would be reading poetry and prose, whatever we wanted, with everyone taking turns. We could later discuss what was read or pose any questions. But the main point was for us to hear real Russian every day, and to speak it.

One might have thought that there was nothing dangerous or difficult in our lives at all, and that the main problem was that Dagmara and I had stopped saying "take it" correctly. But—oh, the almighty power of shifting accents—we were indeed distracted from the dangerous and the difficult, preoccupied with something completely different.

I remember these winter evenings as endless and charming ones. During the day we faced our defenselessness and homelessness. In our sorry hut, never fit for permanent habitation, it was crowded and cold. There was not enough food or clothing; there was just so much household work. Of course, adults did most of it, but we had to help out too—going to the steppe for firewood, carrying water, cleaning, and washing laundry. I had already learned how to sew and patch holes, and spent hours engaged in this work, so boring, but so necessary for us. Sometimes people visited, and the news would always be alarming. We lived under pressure, which by tacit agreement was not discussed. But it kept intensifying.

The evenings were our only escape. The stove was lit. We would shove a whole tumbleweed inside, and through each crack in the stove red stripes of fire flashed. Their reflections danced feverishly across the walls. We put dry corn seeds—our main delicacy—on the hot stove. (Only the "makukha"—the oilcake left over from sunflower seeds after the oil had been squeezed out—was better.) The seeds were jumping up and down, exploding with a pop—now they were excellent hot nuts. Mama was mixing dough for tomorrow's bread.

A broiler lamp, just like the ones from our bomb shelter in Leningrad, its wick made from strands of old cords, would be lit. The big wooden table would already be washed clean and swept dry, everything but the books taken off it.

Somehow, though we read "The Captain's Daughter," "The Queen of Spades," *Evenings on a Farmstead Near Dikan'ka*, and long passages from *Dead Souls*, poetry ended up in first place. And perhaps Pushkin and Gogol received such preference because their prose did not sound prosaic at all: Gogol's was unabashedly lyrical; Pushkin's was more veiled, and thus even more seductive:

At ten o'clock in the evening he was already standing under the countess' window. The weather was terrible: the wind howled, wet snowflakes descended upon him; the lanterns beaconed weakly; streets were empty. Rarely a cart driver would trudge by on his skinny horse, searching for a late fare. Hermann stood wearing just his suit jacket, not feeling either wind or snow.

Consider this: Every time we read that passage, snow and wind would pound the window above the table, as if summoned by an incantation. But they no longer brought sadness, as they had before. Hypnotized by Pushkin, the forces of nature were merely obeying his storyline and accompanying it.

There was an ominous beauty in their howl beyond the window, a beauty completely liberated from the storm's oppressive force. What wild hurricanes of snow and ghosts swirled above our hut!

When my turn came, I read "The Demons" most often:

Clouds race, clouds spin
The invisible moon
Is illuminating the flying snow.
Turbid sky, turbid night . . .
Devils racing, swarm by swarm
In the boundless heights above
And their plaintive squeals and howls
Are harrowing my heart.

It's no wonder that by reading "The Queen of Spades" we were summoning snowstorms and hurricanes—there is indeed some magical force inside a man who could imagine this wild, spinning, moaning chaos in September, when outside his house in Boldino the quiet golden autumn was barely beginning. And for me it was an undeniable axiom that "one can stop the sun with a word and one can capture cities with a word." Didn't I see that myself, when a word unleashed forces of nature and sent them off to wreak havoc above the dark steppe?

For us, only Gogol could come close to Pushkin. Our affection for him lay in our incessant recognition: we were living amidst the places he wrote about. Solokha, Levko, and Katerina were speaking the same language, with the same flexible intonations, as the Cossack women in Kuschevka. We recognized the white huts behind woven fences and poplars under the moonlight. And the chimney through which the Devil crawled on Christmas night was almost identical to ours. Gogol's miracles occurred in huts just like ours, in a world whose every detail was familiar. So for us children, they acquired undeniable veracity—we were unable to consider them fictions.

Chilling scenes from "A Terrible Vengeance" or "St. John's Eve" would nearly inspire me to hallucinations: the tiny Ivas, covered with a sheet, whose head must be severed for the treasures to be captured. And I was not easily frightened by nature. Before the war, it would be told in our family with laughter how one acquaintance had said: "Galina Aleksandrovna made a mistake when she gave birth to Elena as a girl." This stayed with me for a long time. "Mama, maybe you really did make a mistake?" I would pester her. "I think I *am* a boy! Really, why did you all decide that I am a girl?" I was not afraid to walk the night steppe alone. But after Gogol, if I opened the door into the cold, empty middle room in the evening, the slightest shadow on the wall turned into an awful scene: an infant's figure covered with a blinding phosphorescent sheet, and a hunchbacked witch with piercing eyes reaching out with her bony hand, to the infant and to me at once, a hand that stretched and grew, its fingers writhing . . . I would jump back in horror, clutching the door behind me.

Only from Gogol did we find out that ordinary things,

things we had seen hundreds of times, could contain deep mysteries and conceal the invisible. A young lady or a black cat could turn out to be a sorcerer. Down the same road where a bunch of laughing young lads had just walked, an old witch was now speeding on top of Homa Brut, clutching his wooden shoulders. So who knew? Maybe the Yeia, under its reeds and families of ducks, was only pretending to be a lazy shallow river. Maybe pale young ladies with blind eyes would emerge from it at night to do a folk dance in the same field where I took horses out to pasture.

And yesterday afternoon, when the snowstorm died down and the sun came out, eerie howls came from where the trail to the Fourth Subdivision had been before the snowfall. "Those are wolves," Mama said. "In winter they are hungry, so they come closer to the houses." And indeed, something resembling a big, dark dog stopped not far from our hut and stood patiently and motionlessly, totally unlike a dog, watching us with a stubborn fixed stare. Could it really be a wolf? Are those really wolves whose drawling songs and sobs I hear when I can't fall asleep at night?

I would rise up from my bench near the stove, captivated by both fear and the joy of proximity to this menacing magic, separated from me only by the clay wall of an old hut. For wolves are the premier disguise artists—in reality they are not wolves at all, but someone else, you never know who! Remember Count Alexei Tolstoy's description of their surreptitious single-file entry into a sleeping village in "Wolves":

Seven wolves march boldly,
And ahead of them marches
The eighth wolf with white fur,
And the mysterious parade
Is concluded by a ninth,
He of the bloody foot
Who walks behind them with a limp.

They walk around yards and churches ("their eyes like candles, their teeth sharper than awls"), and nobody will come out to challenge them. Only one thing can help: an ancient incantation—a strange ritual with thirteen bullets and a goat's fur—and you cannot miss! And only then, then . . .

In the village, when the sleeping
Are all awakened by the cock
You will see lying there bodies
Of nine dead old women
A gray-haired one in front
And a lame one in the back
All in blood . . . May God help us!

The howl was no longer a howl, but rather a profound moan of suffering. I hugged the still-warm stove even closer— it too represented magic and protection. It seemed that we were alone under an invisible shield on an island, in the middle of the limitless, snow-covered steppe, and something else, which had no name but was the most awesome force of all, was breaking through with these moans. And that supreme force was also tormented by something, and was also complaining— sometimes with fury, sometimes with exhaustion, getting tired of its grief . . .

In the mornings I would go out into the yard where snow had fallen from midnight until dawn. Mama, who usually got up before everyone, had already created little trails through the snowdrifts to the well, the stable, and the barn full of hay, straw, and firewood. They were the only travel routes. I would stop at the very edge of the yard. This was no longer the steppe that had knocked on our window so stubbornly and ominously throughout the night. All the voices, shadows, and fears of the night were covered now with deep snow.

The sun was shining brilliantly, the snow was bright beneath it. There was not a single living being, or even a single dry piece of grass, among this whole blinding expanse. But no, suddenly something emerged from far off and was rapidly approaching me. Something alive, but unreal. Supernaturally not needing any trails, it was speeding straight over the snow, not growing larger or smaller, and remaining unrecognizable inside a cloud of shiny snowflakes.

Then it was almost next to me, and I recognized . . . a tumbleweed. In the fall, when we wandered through the steppe grass, laid low by the rains, we searched everywhere for these round dense bushes. When they dried, they were the best fuel for our stove. They were attached to the ground only by one straight stem, which could be snapped by a mere gust of wind. But this one had held out stubbornly, awaiting a night snowstorm and the whitened steppe. And now it was not a bush but a small comet, carefree and unstoppable, racing above the snowdrifts and sweeping clouds of brilliant cold, white dust with its tail. It had no fancy for visiting our yard, but as it flew past, it smacked a snow pile right next to me as a farewell gesture. An explosion of light dry snow covered me from my headscarf to my boots.

So slick and accurate was this prank that I couldn't help laughing. To hear my own laughter was sudden and unusual—from my own surprise I understood that all of us hardly ever laughed.

The tumbleweed was already flashing far across the snow, but I followed it with my eyes. It had visited us only for a moment just to play a friendly trick and make me laugh. To remind me that this too is part of life: carefree playfulness, roads open in all directions, complete freedom. And that some day, we too might be entitled to this.

We liked reading *Dead Souls* and *The Inspector General* for a special reason. When I was very little and we still lived in Moscow, Mama had been in love with the theatre. She never missed anything at the Vakhtangov Theatre, or the Malyi Theatre. But her favorite was the Moscow Art Theatre. She had a very sharp memory, and before she read a scene to us, she would tell us who was playing each role. She would describe each actor's tone of voice, and the way he walked when he entered the door. She would show us just how Nozdrev would swing the chair at Chichikov, and would shout passionately, "Beat him!" We all loved it.

I must admit that, at the time, I was more confused than the others. It somehow distracted me to know where Moskvin sat and how he talked. Uncertainty was better. I was very young when I first heard of theatre: Mama was telling someone that she had been to see *The Cherry Orchard*, and that the auditorium was packed. I imagined it like this: Mama sat in a big auditorium full of cherry trees. People walked quietly among the trees, and it was difficult to see their faces in the dark. But I knew they were all beautiful, especially the women in their long dresses. When people met, they spoke quietly, saying good and serious things, judging by their movements and their tilted heads—and then they would part ways, and disappear behind the blooming trees. I remembered how nice it was to wake up when Mama returned from the theatre late at night. She would bend down over my tiny bed, beautifully dressed, with shiny eyes, smelling wonderful (it must have been that cherry orchard smell, of course). She would smile and tell me about Tiltil and Mitil from Maeterlinck's *The Blue Bird*, who fell asleep in a ray of moonlight.

But as I have said, poetry was by far our favorite. After Pushkin, we loved Lermontov and Nekrasov best. Here we did not stray much from the traditional preferences of ordinary Russian intellectuals of the past century. And from its first words, it was "The Pedlars" that made me fall in love. The very first lines hypnotized me, but why? Nothing had happened yet; someone had simply begun to drawl a wild sly song. And it wasn't a free Cossack from Zaporozhie singing, or even a coachman on a troika, but a country-boy salesman tramping down the road with his box of fabrics, belts, and ribbons. What did I care about how he made his living? No words, spoken or written, had yet infected me with such happiness. To walk in the countryside, to take a deep breath of fresh air, and to sing as loudly as I could—that was all that mattered! I had just returned to life! I was hesitant, and didn't yet trust this life, but this wide-sweeping, unabashed taste of freedom was like a potent drink, making my head spin.

> I'll come out in a tall rye field
> And wait there till nightfall,
> But if I see a black-eyed beauty
> I'll pull out all my goodies.

And the story played out like flashing reflections in a rushing creek, the spinning rhythm never slowing, always speeding somewhere ahead. And as the pace quickened, it was easier and easier to breathe—even when the incredible catastrophe happened, the words kept me racing on without looking back. It was terrible and stunning in its improbability: All had ended, but as if not noticing Ivan's death, the rhymes kept weaving the melody they had started.

> Almost at once thundered
> Two rifle barrels.
> Ivan falls without a word.
> And the screaming old man crumbles.
> Later that evening in a bar
> The forest ranger laughs and boasts.

I would choke up at this point, when Ivan's life is severed from his song. So cruel was this blow that the rest of the poem would only reach me as if from afar. I would jump up from the bench and go to a dark spot behind the stove. So what about Katya now, I would think in despair. What will happen to her?

Later, in bed, I would find it difficult to sleep. But the next evening, I would again ask Mama to read "The Pedlars." I could never bring myself to read it aloud, not a single line.

THE WINTER CONTINUED, and while our evenings reading around the broiler lamp helped to make it colorful, something unkind was more and more visibly approaching. Leningrad women we knew visited from other, faraway subdivisions. On such occasions, something was always found for me and Dagmara to do in Aunt Khvenya's room, in the yard, or in the barn. But we both understood that nobody would walk across the frozen steppe, risking an encounter with Germans, just to say hello. Whenever we walked into the room, we would hear only shreds of conversations which would stop immediately: *There's nowhere to run anyway . . . Everybody's on the list, children too . . . Our troops have started an offensive . . . That won't help us now . . .*

Local villagers stopped by too. They had changed noticeably, both in their demeanor toward us and in general. They asked about our lives more often and with more interest, and talked about their own more willingly. Their remarks about the Germans became increasingly hostile. There were constant stories about endless levies and sometimes outright robberies. Any yard could at any minute be visited by a soldier with a submachine gun, or by several soldiers. The Germans were walking around in groups more often, having found that this made a greater impression. Their vocabulary was limited and goal-oriented: "Woman! Pig, chicken, eggs, lard, milk." Sometimes they simply took what they needed, without any words or negotiations. They might take not only food, but any trinket that pleased their eye, like an embroidered towel that hung in a corner under an icon. This was particularly infuriating to the Cossack women—it was no longer the seizure of something necessary, but purely an insulting reminder of the soldiers' unlimited power.

Our former landlady told us, intensely and eloquently, a story about doing her laundry. After she was finished washing, she leaned the empty washbasin against a fence and went to hang the laundry on ropes. Two soldiers were passing by. They glanced inside the yard, evaluated everything with a thrifty look, and took the washbasin without saying a word.

"So I chase after them, 'Damn you, why do you steal from me? What will that washbasin do for you, save you from bullets? Where will I buy another one?' But they said nothing, they just kept walking and laughing, the wicked bastards!"

The locals had a great sense of humor and knew how to use it. Only years later, remembering those funny incidents, did I understand what our storytellers were trying to do. These stories were their barrier against the truly terrible, their way of convincing themselves and others that nothing worse than the idiotic theft of a washbasin really threatened them. In our vegetable-garden brigade, isolated from everything, we really didn't know much. They knew more, yet they remained silent. Not so much for us—for themselves.

Once, when Mama was returning home from the Churakovs' after the Germans had already retreated, she decided to take a shortcut through a field. The path bent around the corner of a large burial mound. When Mama got around it, she saw several people and a dug-up grave. She stopped, stunned. Almost in her path lay a young boy's body, maybe thirteen or fourteen years old. He had been buried without a coffin, but the loose earth had been brushed off his face. The steppe was just beginning to thaw. Mama could not tear her eyes away from the boy's face, totally calm as if he were merely sleeping, sleeping like a child. All the more horrible was this child's sleep when Mama saw his mutilated hands: his fingernails were torn off. The locals told Mama that the Germans tortured him before they shot him—he was suspected of helping some underground guerillas. Was he really helping? Everybody shrugged their shoulders. He didn't say anything under torture (maybe because he had nothing to say), so the Germans grew angry, and shot him. And there, on the other side of the mound, villagers were digging up others—three more already. And why were those killed? Who knows? You know how it was during the Germans' last days. You said something wrong—here's a bullet for you. They shot them here in the steppe, far from other people.

Mama did not go to the other side of the mound. She stayed to help clean up the little body. Exactly a year had passed since she had cleaned another body, that of her firstborn, for the medics' stretcher.

Though the Cossack women kept silent about this, for the most part they spoke more bluntly than the Leningrad women who visited us. And when no adults were around, they didn't duck Dagmara's and my questions. That's how we found out that the commandant's office was preparing lists for mass executions. That all the Leningrader families were included, with no exceptions. This was said severely and calmly. There were locals on the lists too. It would get ugly. There was only one hope—that the Germans would be chased away before the executions could begin.

I felt a dark veil lifted from my eyes, and suddenly a bright shining line pointed at a whole life ahead. Because the Germans might be made to retreat. And because this was being said, and hoped for, by previously estranged people, I had the forgotten feeling of accord, of common hopes and dreams. So really, are they retreating? Maybe, people said. What do you hear? Different things.

Silence hung over the steppe for almost the whole winter. So when I went out into the yard one day and heard an unusual noise in the distance, I stopped in astonishment and slid the headscarf away from my ear. Yes, there it was: a vague roar, and over that at irregular intervals, a sound like dull heavy thunder. This was a time when all children, even ones younger than myself, could tell unerringly a Messerschmitt from a Focke-Wulf by sound alone, not to mention the difference between a bombing raid and an artillery attack. I was from Leningrad.

I ran into the hut. Mama was sewing at the table.

"Mama," I said, hardly able to get a word out. "Mama. Artillery."

Mama raised her head and looked at me, not understanding. Nothing could be heard inside the hut, so far away was the roar.

"Artillery," I repeated colorlessly, my tongue still wooden. "Long range."

Mama grabbed her headscarf and rushed into the yard. For a minute there was no sound, just the usual quiet of the steppe. But then the silence was pierced by a distant, yet distinct, salvo. Then another volley—and behind it came the ominous roar, as if the steppe itself were emitting it from all its hills and snowdrifts.

Mama stood with her head uncovered, her headscarf in her hands. She did not speak or sob, but her entire face was drenched with tears.

Our troops took Kuschevka on February 23, 1943.

⚜

THAT HAPPINESS OF LIBERATION which I had been anticipating, listening to our guests' conversations, was nothing compared to what we actually experienced. Only having rid yourself of a burden do you realize how oppressive it really was. Our whole life, which we had been painstakingly measuring and filling so as not to leave a single opening for emptiness, fear, or despair, was instantly torn to pieces—and how happy we were to destroy its order, to do away with all of our habits! All of us, not just children but adults too, lost our heads. There were no more lessons or readings. We children leaped and screamed in riotous games. We were unstoppable! I would run aimlessly down a trail, or straight into the steppe across the snow. The feelings of freedom and safety, which I was experiencing for the first, yes, the first time in my life (my prewar childhood now seemed to be somebody else's life, not mine), brought uncontrollable exhilaration. I can go where I want, when I want!

The doors of our hut never closed. All the Leningraders, scattered across sprawling subdivisions, were now making the rounds to each other's houses to get their fill of talk. How loudly we all spoke now, how much we laughed! Visitors would take treats out of their bags: bread wrapped in a towel, a piece of salted lard, and once (we froze in admiration) a trophy can of meat received as a gift from our soldiers. Mama and Yeliza-veta Nikolayevna, not wanting to be outdone, would cover the table with everything we had in the house. Nobody thought about tomorrow anymore, no more scrupulously measuring the flour left in our little bag, wondering if it could be made to last for three days.

Actually, people did think and talk about tomorrow constantly, but in another sense. A return to Leningrad seemed to all of us not only probable, but imminent. One guest after another spoke of what they planned to find at home, remembering every shelf on their walls and the view from their windows. "Mine look right over the Fontanka River!" Not a single doubt was permitted to be cast over these rosy reminiscences. The Blockade was hardly ever mentioned. It seemed forever overshadowed by the new trials of the occupation, and it appeared obvious now that nothing more difficult was left ahead. Nobody wanted to think that, perhaps, the house on the banks of the Fontanka was now just piles of bricks and broken glass. I know well that some of our guests never did make it back to Leningrad—even though their house on the Fontanka or the Obvodnyi Canal had perhaps survived, and even if all the shelves were still along the walls.

We were also visited by the collective farmers much more often now. They would bring week-old newspapers, recount what news they had heard on the radio, and ask Mama questions about geography so they could understand the latest bulletin from the front. Now we all knew who had a husband, a nephew, or a son at the front; who had a wound or shell shock; who had received how many medals. Then the triangular envelopes began to appear—letters from the front. The farmers brought them to Mama to be read. I don't think all these Cossack women were really illiterate; this ritual gave them profound pleasure. A guest would give Mama a triangle: "Please read, Leksandrovna." Then the guest would slowly sit down at the table and put her hands on her knees, or prop up her scarved head. She would not change this posture until the reading was done, sitting quietly, concentrating, while Mama read slowly and accurately. Then she would demand clarifications: What was that about a hospital? And where the lines were crossed out, that is censorship? What came before that censored part? There's no way you can read what is crossed out. Each letter was thus read in its entirety, segment by segment, no less than three times—even the obligatory regards to "Uncle Semyon and Aunt Ganna," which sometimes took up several lines.

Then an even more complex and important ceremony would begin: composing the reply. Mama was handed a precious clean sheet of paper, and a long discussion ensued about what should be written. The task was quite a challenging one: Mama would listen to a lengthy narrative about the health and affairs of the entire family and all their relatives, about what they were planning to plant and when, about the fact that Manka the Cow gave birth last week to a little bull calf; about how the weather is hotter than it had been in five years and the spring in the little valley had dried up. All this had to be squeezed onto the two sides of one sheet, leaving space for the military address.

I enjoyed listening to these slow recitatives of family and village news, watching them gradually be shaped into ancient formulas resembling a traditional folk song. Each woman knew instinctively how to do this. She had learned it from her mother and her grandmother. The news about the family and relatives, about the spring and Manka the Cow, was almost hidden now under the firmly woven pattern of this ancient tapestry. But perhaps this was what the triangle's addressee needed most: to

hear the unswerving Kuban village intonation, the habitual say-
ings and the litanies of regards from relatives and neighbors, as
all Cossacks sent to war would hear them from one century to
the next, and find in this predictable pattern a confirmation
that everything at home was okay.

Once, after the Germans had left, Dagmara and I were sent
on an errand to a subdivision across the river. Our mothers told
us it was another Leningrad family from our train, but Dagmara and I could not remember them. We got up, ate our
breakfast, and set out into the steppe.

It was a long trek, and this only made us happier. We still
felt the novelty of freedom and safety. Now, from this bright
present, we were looking back at the recent past almost with
horror. How had we done it? How did we stand our cloistered
life, intensely concentrating on any sound from the road, looking through a peephole at a German officer in the yard, not
meeting anyone?

The morning was beautiful. Spring was only beginning,
the air was fresh and brisk. A crisp crunch came from the frosty
puddles whose ice crackled under our feet, and we walked to
this melody.

Dagmara was a serious and sensible girl. I liked her a lot,
and might have liked her even more if I hadn't felt a subtle bite
of jealousy. Mama constantly praised her and held her up as a
role model for me. I knew in fact that this was deserved—
Dagmara would willingly do any chore, and was preoccupied
with Nirs as much if not more than Yelizaveta Nikolayevna
herself. Her character was already molded: calm, patient, and

fair. Of course she was a good influence on me. But I would never acknowledge it aloud. Instead, I would often respond to Mama with "Not everyone can be so kind!" Sometimes I would agree that Dagmara was indeed better than I, but only because she was older. Obviously, virtue must grow with age. See, a year ago I didn't know how to patch my socks, but now I do. Earlier I didn't have enough patience, and now I do. When I grow up, like Dagmara, I might become even more orderly than she. Here Mama could not stand it any longer and would begin to laugh out loud. And I would soon join in the laughter.

How good it was to walk so far like this. Singing, we crossed the river on an unfinished bridge. And soon we were walking past huts, woven fences, and cherry orchards, still without leaves but already smelling of spring.

But the most wonderful thing was the noise and variety of voices. We had lived in silence and solitude, and here everything bustled happily all around us. Birds were outsinging each other as they jumped between cherry branches. A flock of geese ran up to us near a fence, hissing and cackling indignantly. Dogs behind each gate were alerting the whole subdivision that strangers were about, so two curious housewives poked their heads out, asked who we wanted to see, and showed us the way. Somewhere nearby a gang of children was noisily playing— maybe we could play together! And in every wide-open barn something was mooing, or grunting, or squawking.

We were shown to a hut a little out of the way. At home we had heard the story that the hut had been left empty for some reason, and that the Leningrad women whom we were going to visit had been allowed to live there. Dagmara and I looked this unusual place over from the gate with a special curiosity. The women had good luck. It was a real house!

"That's what they call destiny's darlings," Dagmara said. She went up to the door and knocked. No response. She waited for quite a while, then looked back at me.

"You did it too quietly," I said.

"Out of respect for the darlings," she explained. "We can try louder now."

Louder didn't help either. Nobody was opening the door, and no sound could be heard from within. We looked at each other.

"They're probably in the garden," I suggested.

I quickly went around the corner to the garden. Nobody. The land had not been shoveled yet. A lone red chicken was digging in the soil.

"What a puzzle," I said when I returned. "Are there houses like The Flying Dutchman and The Mysterious Starship?"

"Come on now." Dagmara the realist got angry and shook the door handle. "They must've left."

"Last try," I proposed and loudly knocked on the windowpane. And then some small voice was heard from within. Followed by a pause and hasty footsteps.

"Who are you?" asked a woman's voice from behind the door.

"We are from Yelizaveta Nikolayevna's and Galina Aleksandrovna's," Dagmara said loudly. "From the vegetable-garden brigade."

The voice behind the door became happy and hurried, we heard movement inside, and finally the door opened. In the doorway stood a woman who could have been either 25 or 40 years old. (Dagmara later said, "Approximately thirty-two.") Her appearance was bizarre. She was completely disheveled, her hair falling straight over her face, which was swollen from sleep. Her eyes were blinking chaotically, and a coat was tossed over her shoulders. She wore only a nightshirt underneath. But her voice was very welcoming.

"My darlings, you walked so far! And why so early? Well, come on in, why stand out in the cold?"

I said that it was neither far nor cold, and Dagmara added that it was eleven o'clock already. Then we were both simultaneously embarrassed not to have greeted her properly, but she was already welcoming us inside.

"Come in already! You must be tired, have a seat."

Inside the hut, we were hit by a wave of stale, heavy, sour air. There were two unkempt beds in the room. And on one of them a young woman was sitting and getting dressed as she looked us over. She nodded to us, still half asleep, and we greeted her. The table near the window was full of dirty dishes, and the stove was also full of piled dishes and pots. The lady tried to sit us down, but both stools were covered with socks and skirts and shirts. There was a bench under the window, in a spot of bright sun, somewhat less littered with clothes. Dagmara sat down on it, but got back up quickly and, making an incomprehensible gesture to me, began to talk business with the lady.

I had settled myself on the same bench. But Dagmara backed up toward me and, continuing her conversation, pulled my sleeve. I looked up at her, but her back was still turned. Yet she stubbornly pulled my sleeve again. Did I have to get up? Why was she being so bossy?

Then she turned around to me and quickly motioned toward the clothes on the bench. I looked over, and at first didn't see anything. Then it seemed . . . I knew that I wasn't mistaken and jumped to my feet. Across a crumpled sweater which lay next to me, fat gray lice were swarming.

Suddenly our past, the months on the train, seemed to tighten around my throat. We had lain together like sardines on wooden bunks and straw, falling asleep with the living and waking up with the dead. These same lice, exactly the same, were crawling everywhere. But since then . . . here these people had a well and a stove! How could they live this way?

I could suddenly smell the heavy, suffocating stench of dirty clothes, unwashed bodies, and the stinking, rotting, never-healing lesions that almost all of us were covered with by the time we got off the train. I had lesion scars on my head and hands. An abscess opened up on Mama's thumb. Every day, though she cleaned out the dead tissue, more and more of her white bone was visible, and the decay kept crawling lower. One morning Mama washed her finger, as always, and examined the abscess. Then she quietly took the sharpest knife around, turned aside, laid her finger on a board, and chopped off the upper half. Then she silently wrapped up the wound. Miraculously, it healed.

All this, previously suppressed during our life under occupation, now began to close in on me. The railcar, the lesions, lice, and death . . . No, I don't want this! This is over, there is no train!

Dagmara suddenly yanked my hand.

"Oh dear, we left your gate open, and there's a dog out there. Lena, do go close it, quickly!"

I dashed out into the yard and through the gate, gulping down the fresh air. Very soon Dagmara emerged as well.

We walked in silence for a while. A long while.

"Dagmara, why do they live like that?"

"Everybody lives in their own way."

"And where do they get food?"

"They brought lots of things to barter. They say that might last them almost until autumn. And then they'll see. They say they'll probably go back to Leningrad . . ."

"And do they have books?"

"I didn't notice any. Did you?"

"So how do they . . . What do they do in the evenings?"

"Play cards."

"Cards?"

"Yeah. Poker. Or 'drunk idiot.' "

Again we walked silently.

"Dagmara!"

"Yes, what?"

"If they could still live like that . . . maybe we could too?"

"No. We could not."

She said this very confidently, without any reflection.

"Why not?"

This time she thought for a while.

"If we could live like that, then we would have lived like that. And since we live differently, that means we cannot live like that."

I liked the sound of this, and felt great respect for Dagmara's logic. So that's what solving advanced math problems does: Now the person is able to answer any question. But I couldn't quite let go.

"So why couldn't we?"

"Here you go again, 'Why, why?' It's just that people are different. Our mothers are not like these people. They like order."

No, this time she did not think enough. It was true, they did like order. But why do some like it and some not? I remembered our life in Leningrad, where Mama was far from a naturally orderly person with a rule and a place for everything. Aunt Talya—she was such a person. I could picture her coming to visit us, stopping in the middle of the room to ask, in a patient and carefully subservient voice, "Might someone advise me where in this house I may sit down?"

Indeed, there really was no place to sit. On one corner of the sofa was Tanya, looking at the pictures in Marshak's *The Circus*:

I am the beautiful Miss Jenny
I am galloping around the arena
Hip-hop, hip-hop
In my pink saddle!

In the other corner lay Mama's sewing, and the middle was very pompously presided over by the neighbors' fat striped cat. Two chairs were pulled together, on which Vadik and I were assembling something from our toy construction kit. On a third chair several of my books were piled up; the fourth was occupied by Vadik's jacket and Mama's apron. Only one chair was serving its true purpose—Grandma was sitting on it by the table, cleaning apples for a pie.

Aunt Talya courageously blazed a trail toward the sofa.

"I understand, of course, that I am violating the manners of this household, but I feel that I have no choice. May this chair not be moved aside? Ah, you're assembling a toy on it. And this one? There are books on it. Whose books are they? Yours, Lenochka? And you are reading all three at once? Let us assume so. But now you are not reading, but building something—so perhaps the books might find a better place on a bookshelf? Vadik, is that your jacket? Why is it here and not on a hanger? And once again you have this shady cat here. Are you sure he has no diseases?"

But here, at the vegetable-garden brigade, Mama was almost more uptight than Aunt Talya. Why was she constantly telling me to sweep the floor one more time? The clay walls were all cracked and crumbling, as was the old stove, and clay crumbs were always all over the floor no matter what you did.

"This is like the Danaides' Labor!" I once obstinately declared, armed with my limited knowledge of mythology. "How much can you do? The cleanliness will only last for a half-hour, and then it will be just like it was before I swept up."

"Well, first of all, not a half-hour but about three hours. And then, is it really that hard for you? Look how many potatoes Dagmara has already cleaned. I think sweeping is a lot easier."

"There is utility in potatoes. We will eat them. But what is the utility in this? I keep sweeping, and the walls keep crumbling."

"This is our home. Good or bad, it has saved us all this winter. And since it took care of us, we may want to take care of it. We live here, therefore we are responsible for it."

"To whom are we responsible?"

"To ourselves. That might be the most important thing—to be responsible to oneself."

I would sigh and pick up a broom. Why respond? All right, it's not so hard, I'll sweep up.

Dinner was already prepared by the time Dagmara and I made it back to the house. We opened the door, and for the first time I realized how cheery, cozy, and nice our home was. How ceremoniously our books stood on a chest covered with an embroidered towel. How shiny the washed pans were on the stove, how white the curtain was, how brightly the sun was smiling through a clean windowpane. And how clean and smooth the floor was.

Nirs was sitting at the table, where the dishes and spoons were already set out and the bread sliced. He was hammering the table with his spoon and screaming happily, "Let's eat, let's eat! Hip-hop, hip-hop! Eat!"

Dagmara and I were very hungry. Still, as we hurriedly

swallowed our hot borscht, we couldn't stop telling our story. Yelizaveta Nikolayevna was indignant.

"It's terrible how low people can sink! And these are Leningraders, can you imagine? Probably completely uneducated. But it's a good lesson for you. At least you will value what is being done for you in our home. Because you are spoiled by our order, and do not understand how much effort it requires of Galina Aleksandrovna and me. But now you've been able to evaluate the difference. You see what depths people can reach!"

We were so flattered by our story's popularity that we began to tell it again, now with new details, increasingly drawn into the importance of our prosecutorial role.

"They probably don't wash dishes for several days! It couldn't be piled up so high from just one day. And there was a whole pile of garbage near the stove."

I did not notice right away that Mama was not participating in the conversation. She kept going off and fidgeting by the stove. A couple of times she glanced at me and Dagmara with a fixed stare, but said nothing. My tales began losing steam, and I started feeling a vague unease.

After dinner she got up to go out, saying it was time to milk the cow since Aunt Khvenya had been sick in bed all day. It seemed a bit early to milk the cow, still, I volunteered to help her.

I first visited my friends, the horses, with some hay. Then I made another trip for the cow. When I returned to the stable with a stack of hay, Mama had already washed Brownie's udder with warm water, and wiped it dry with a soft towel. Now, as always before milking her, Mama was talking softly to her and caressing her head and neck. Brownie was listening, looking content and dignified. The stable was warm and lit by a lantern on the windowsill. Mama placed a polished bucket under the cow's udder and sat down on an old box in front of it. But I could not wait and did not let her begin.

"Mama!"

"Yes?"

"Mama, were we saying something that was not right?"

Mama looked pensive.

"Hmm, how can I put it? Maybe right. But . . ."

"But what?"

"I couldn't talk like that."

"Why?"

"Because I feel very sorry for those women. Yes, it's very bad, what you saw there. But don't be so . . . overconfident. I find it very difficult to condemn them."

"Why?"

"Because I know well what they have lived through. We all have a common past. You still do not fully understand what we have all endured. You will later. But you do remember. You remember the railcar, right?" I nodded. "You remember how crippled we all were—with frostbite, with diarrhea, with lesions?"

Mama's hands lay on her knees, on top of the apron. I looked at her mutilated finger. Mama noticed and slid her hand inside a pocket.

"Parts of our bodies died. In some people, much worse,

parts of their souls died. How do we know how many coffins those women had? To them, it might seem that life has nothing more to offer. If they return to Leningrad, they might resume their previous . . . almost-normal life. But for them it will be much more difficult."

Mama paused.

"Can you understand? People drift away from the flow, and if they let some time lapse, it's much more difficult to come back to the old spot. So little depends on us!"

The lantern's flames were sending sharp and trembling shadows everywhere. A strange and unusual expression of near-despair flashed across Mama's face.

"But when something does depend on us, even the slightest trifle—you cannot miss any chances. Every minute you must paddle against the current. Everything is needed: to wash the dishes, to read books, to study the multiplication table, to sweep the floor. And then, one sunny day, it turns out that we have survived, and survived as human beings. You understand? As human beings. And now let's end all talk. Look at Brownie, she's getting anxious. She's afraid we have given up on milking her."

Brownie was indeed turning toward us and wagging her tail delicately, yet with some annoyance.

I walked out to the stable's threshold. It was already completely dark, the stars were out, and the air was growing colder. Silence surrounded me, except behind my back where I could hear the steady ringing of tight streams of milk as they hit the bucket's wall. I thought about the two women playing cards on the other side of the Yeia. But now, from here, their faces did not seem lifeless and sleepy to me. I could see that they were only bitter and tired, as we all had once been. Repentance and embarrassment burned me inside. But I also felt relief. Why, I did not know.

⚜

AS SOON AS the Germans left, Mama enrolled me in the nearest school. It was only about two kilometers away, just on the other side of the Yeia, almost directly across from us. I could even see the building from home, until the cherry trees hid it from late spring until autumn. But the closest bridge (and even this one was unfinished) was so far that I had to make a long hook through the steppe, crossing a valley, then the river, and then walking the shoreline along a farmstead.

My preparation for school was a true holiday. Mama sewed a bookbag for me from an old towel and covered it with a beautiful embroidered basket of flowers. My two dresses were patched up, ironed, and also embroidered with something new. My shoes were another story, but these were not times in which to pay attention to such things. Though of course, I had to think about this when it was cold. But from frost until frost I ran around barefoot, and even the thin morning ice on the muddy road did not bother me. When the cold weather ended I would leave the hut barefoot in the morning, and walk most of the way to school. Only after crossing the river would I descend to the water, thoroughly wash my feet (they would dry immediately in the sun) and put on my old shoes. I would walk the last leg of the trip with dignity, as if it were a parade, and would enter the school a well-groomed girl, well-dressed, with a nice bag. That's how I imagined myself.

It is hard to describe the ardent hope with which I anticipated school. Chekhov's three sisters did not dream about Moscow as much as I dreamed about school. For me too, it seemed that everything necessary was represented by a single thing, the one key that would open all doors. I don't know what happened to the sisters, the curtain falls before they reach Moscow. Vera Figner, whose writings I loved as an adolescent, thinks that "either the all-consuming depression or the feisty spirit is all inside the person," and that the three sisters will remain trapped in boredom and decay in Moscow just as they were in the province.

As for myself, I was immediately, clearly, and irreversibly disillusioned. It was naïve and unjust for me to feel this way, and even then I suspected this deep inside. Maybe I had expected too much. But why did this disappointment hurt me so much when I was so easily tolerant of everything else that wasn't quite "right" here?

It was so unlike what I wanted. I could not forget the school that Vadik had attended—School No. 107 on our Vyborgskaya Street. It occupied a building of several stories, with big windows and a spectacular front door. Inside were a bright, glamorous staircase, wide hallways, and doors that opened into spacious classrooms, crisscrossed by straight rows of desks. All the walls were decorated with maps, tables, blueprints, bookshelves, flowers, and stuffed birds and animals.

I knew, of course, that none of this could exist in a small village school. But I felt a pang of disappointment still, after happily greeting everyone, when I asked the other children which grade this was. "We're all together," I was told. The whole school fit into one room. To the left, by the window, were the first-graders. And to the right, seniority grew to sixth or seventh grade. All together, there were about fifteen kids. Some grades did not exist at all, if there was no one of the requisite age in the nearby subdivisions. One teacher—a lively, friendly young woman—taught everyone simultaneously. She would assign a problem to one grade and, while they were solving it, order another grade to open their books to such-and-such a page and do such-and-such exercises. While those grades dipped their pens in ink bottles, scraping their bottoms (there was never enough ink), she would explain a lesson to yet another grade or would begin a quiz.

It was much like Mama's school at the vegetable-garden brigade. Our home school was quieter and more disciplined though, because there were fewer of us there. In one corner a stove burned (when I began classes, the frosts still held), and the student in charge had to get up from time to time and toss in more firewood. On the way, of course, he would yank someone's sleeve, and she would then retaliate by tripping him. If hot coals fell out of the stove door, three or four delighted kids would race to the stove, and a melee would ensue. During a lesson, somebody who had shown up unprepared would stutter a response while the answer was being whispered to him from all grades at once. I immediately appreciated the fact that at least this place was not boring.

A big issue arose as to which grade I should be placed in. In Russian, history, and geography I could have sat in fourth grade, but in arithmetic I could not go above third grade. Worst of all, I could barely write. True, after the Germans left we could already afford to buy ourselves paper from time to time, but this had only been for a matter of weeks. After much vacillation, the teacher decided to enroll me in first grade, because there was no second or third grade at the school. That became the main source of my frustration: I had nothing to do there except draw sticks to learn how to write; I wasn't even called upon to read by syllables or subtract two from seven. There was only one thing left to do: to join the battle near the stove and show others how the ancient Russian warriors struggled with the Mongols, or to use the occasion to tease Volodya Prozenko about his long nose.

My second disappointment was that my hopes of finding some friends were quickly frustrated. Kids were friendly, and so was I, but still something did not mesh. There was almost nobody my age, most of them were older, but that was not the main problem. Somehow, I could find nothing to talk about with the Cossack girls. At nine or ten, they had already become junior housewives in their families and were helping around the house a great deal. So was I. But there were few similarities between my scant dormitory subsistence at the vegetable-garden brigade and the concerns of these thrifty and orderly girls, who knew how to pickle lard; skim cream from milk; operate a separator; whip butter; and feed geese, chickens, and pigs. And when home matters came up, a hint of superiority would glimmer in these girls—so I tried to stay clear of this topic. But there weren't really any others. They disliked books and were interested in reports from the front. All that occupied them, besides housework, were their relatives and neighbors. But nothing that happened with the Danilenkos, the Okhrimenkos, or the Stashuks—none of whom I knew—concerned me at all. And there was nothing I could offer in the endless discussions of these families' problems.

So that left the boys. At first I was hopeful. I could discuss the military situation with them, and generally they were well-informed. They knew which places on the Yeia had the strongest ice now, and promised to show me (the other girls looked askance at this). They also knew where the Yeia would dry up in the summer, where there would be some crayfish to catch. When they heard that in the summer I would be taking horses to pasture, they were slightly surprised (the girls again fell silent), but offered very useful advice right away: where the grass was better, where water could be found, where I should watch out for snakes. They were always chewing something, and I asked what it was. They showed me yellow transparent lumps of sticky, aromatic gum—tar from the sunny sides of cherry trees. Will you show me where? Sure, why not.

Soon though, I noticed that these conversations were somehow violating an important and unfamiliar code. When I paid more attention, I realized what it was: Girls and boys kept to themselves. They had good relations, cracking jokes with each other, but long conversations between the genders were not the norm. This was incomprehensible to me, so I asked the girls about it. They were even more puzzled by such incomprehension: Obviously, boys have their lives and girls have theirs. And why wouldn't a girl talk to a boy about something? Sure, she can go ahead and talk, but then she's a "boy-chaser." What's a boy-chaser? A girl who chases after boys.

Strange as it was to me, at least now it was clear. And I began to conduct myself with boys the same way the rest of the girls did. Even though I was longing to learn more about the Yeia, about snakes and turtles, and about what was burrowing in the sand on the cliff by the old bridge, I had learned not to mess with the village code.

Strangely, I was reminded of that code many years later, in another remote village, this time in the Volosovsky Region near Leningrad. We university students had been living there for a month, "assigned to potatoes"—helping out in a particularly stormy autumn with a scant collective-farming harvest. Our group of friends, archeologists and art historians, was settled in a lonely old woman's house. Her children and grandchildren had left the village hopelessly for the big city, and she was all alone. Nice and sociable by nature, she was missing her family and was delighted by our noisy invasion. Actually, almost every house in the village was just as deserted. Our classmate from East Germany, an historian named Hans (who was obviously sent to the collective farm through some oversight by the authorities), kept approaching us, one after another, in confusion.

"I do not understand why in Russian villages there are only very old people and very young children," he said.

But we had all seen Russian villages before, and accepted them with the same ease as we accepted long lines in the cities, communal housing, and asinine speeches at political meetings. Of course all these things would disappear in two or three years, and due to their nature as relics of the past they did not deserve even indignation, only humor. It's difficult to say whether our infantile optimism was a reflection of Khrushchev's thaw or just a disease that afflicts a certain age group, like chicken pox. But we were full of joie de vivre, joking as we paced the flooded potato fields in thigh-high boots, with still enough energy to stay up in the evenings to visit and to debate the merits of Peter the Great's reforms, of Shamil, or of an exhibit from the Louvre at the Hermitage.

One evening, someone came up with the idea to organize a dance in the empty club of the village Soviet. Some friends came by to invite us, and everybody agreed but me. I just didn't feel like it. I had been waiting all day to sit down in the evening and read poetry—I had just discovered the "Silver Age." And the sunset was incredible. Gray-black clouds were piling on top of each other, pierced by the last rays of the day. Below them, and above the black empty field and the spiky ridge of a fir forest, a bright stripe extended, like a thin blade, separating the two dark abysses. It was like a prologue of caution against the unknown which lay behind the horizon.

I was relishing my time alone, sitting on the porch with a book. The old woman, our hostess, walked by just then. She stopped when she saw me.

"I like you, Elena."

I was so surprised that I even lowered my book.

"Why is that?"

Maybe I, still mindful of our life at the vegetable-garden brigade, had more often realized that she needed help with things like bringing in firewood or water. Or perhaps it was simply that I had given her some sweets for her tea that Mama had sent from the city? But it was nothing like that. She was completely candid.

"Because you don't chase after the lads."

I burst out laughing. But under a suddenly disapproving gaze (such laughter was also a violation of the code) I stifled my amusement and listened to the entire lecture. A girl must have pride. Somebody asks her out and she runs off with him right away? On the next day the boy will run off too, only in the other direction. No, she must make him keep coming and asking. I really wanted to tell her that I had only skipped the dance because my book was interesting. But I liked the idea of being the girl with too much pride. I was flattered. Not long before that I had read Montesquieu's theory that climate affects morals. But now I thought, here is proof to the contrary! From the steppe's black soil to the northern swamps, the code was the same. What consistency, despite years and distances.

But the reminder of Kuschevka, having flashed once, was now back. Only now I thought of the differences. In

Kuschevka, this code, which I had just laughed about, was one of the last lines of defense. It was something still left to guard. Everything else had already been taken or lost. Almost no men could be seen, but the young Cossack ladies still walked with quiet dignity. They gazed out with their black eyes beneath straight eyebrows and white headscarves, still refusing to look down. The yards were noisy with boys and girls my age and older, the clay huts were brightly white, and in the gardens mallows were trembling and cherry trees blossomed. Cows mooed in the barns.

On the old lady's farm, I looked out from the porch. A deserted street, covered with black puddles, lay before me, and not a single voice could be heard. Decrepit wooden huts, darkened by steady downpours, sat glum with lightless windows. More than half of them were boarded up. Nobody repaired the crooked fences. Only very old people and very young children, as Hans had noted. But unlike Hans, we knew that little children had been sent here from the city to their grandmas by the sons and daughters who had left, and that they would be taken back when they reached school age. So there was nothing left to guard here. The old code was simply living out its days, like the crooked fence which nobody had needed for a long time now. Like our grandmother hostess, who had nobody in her hut to teach these kind and ancient words about a girl's pride, and so spoke them to me, a random student visitor.

The sky was dimming now. The old village, dying slowly and defenselessly, had almost merged with the blackness of the field and the forest, as if sinking into them and away from life.

For the first time, my childish optimism began to ebb and I had no reply for the advancing gloom—the foreign gloom of a doomed village, of boarded-up huts and empty fields, which was also somehow now mine.

But many years before then, as a child in Kuschevka, I hadn't given much thought to the code. I accepted it as something else I had to live with. Of course I was sad about it. Neither during classes nor in the breaks between them was this the school I had hoped for. That school never existed.

Of course, I wasn't old enough to understand that despite all my wishes, destiny had made me a great, unimaginable gift: years of a childhood that was free, unbridled, and untainted, despite all its hardships. I adored (as many kids do) the idea of school's official and glamorous side: orderly rows of desks, children who stand up at once when the teacher appears, white collars on dark dresses, hands raised in eager expectation. And I was far from understanding that this child's play of the "adult world" was already being used by our government. Grammar schools were becoming the taming ground for future compliant and subordinate Soviet citizens. I was spared all this in my very receptive early childhood. Until I was more than eleven years old, I studied only in makeshift schools where I never heard the words "community," "undertaking," or "Up for the roll-call! Stand at attention!"

I guess I never really became the kind of student I was supposed to become in a real school. Once as an upper-grade girl, I got into an argument with our physics teacher. She suddenly got angry: "How can you talk to me like this? You don't respect me!" I was shocked. I had a great deal of respect for her. She had given me both A's and D's, she was abrupt and uptight, but irreproachably fair. She had a brilliant mind. But I suppose my respect was not expressed in the manner to which she was accustomed. I was indeed unable to feel for my teachers (and in Leningrad we had amazing ones) the unconditional reverence which was prescribed by school law. I did not grace anyone with that reverence, and only fully experienced it, for the first time in my life, when after the university I became a pupil of the last great Hermitage scientist, Vladimir Franzevich Levinson-Lessing.

Perhaps deep in my subconscious, oriented by some compass of childhood intuition, I felt that something was right, for I was very attached to my first school despite it all. After quickly dispensing with my simplistic first-grade assignment, I wouldn't miss a word of what the teacher said to the upper-grade students. That's how I absorbed so many bits of their knowledge about history and botany, so many lists of wonderful-sounding names of mountain ranges and islands. I liked the whole spirit of relationships at the school, which was simple and casual. The upper-grade students, aged fourteen or fifteen, were considered adults pursuant to local custom (especially in wartime, without fathers and older brothers in the house) and conducted themselves with the teacher almost as equals. They all had an innate, weighty dignity. And although I had no close friends of my own, I was friendly with everyone.

It was no surprise, then, that I did not want to miss my lessons for any reason, even in the very worst weather. During frosts or the spring mud, I would get up at daybreak (in bad weather the walk could take two hours), put my notebooks and breakfast in my sack, and head out. Once, this stubbornness almost cost me dearly. Despite the snow and wind, and everyone's opinion that I should stay home, I walked to school. Mama always granted me great discretion in such matters, believing that I could already be responsible for myself.

While school was in session, the weather seemed to improve, but in the late afternoon, it got worse than ever. They offered to let me stay overnight at the school, or to take me to someone else's house, but I refused.

Walking on the trail along the river was not too bad. I was shielded by the high bank, the houses, and fences. But once I reached the rickety bridge, in the middle of the open steppe, everything swirled and raged. A blizzard was beginning. I barely got across the river. But then it got even worse. The cold, the wind, and the snow all grew meaner as if racing each other. The road was buried in snow and was already indistinguishable from the steppe. This was still okay—I firmly knew the direction and was not straying from it, and it made no difference whether I was walking on the road or through the steppe. Everything was blanketed in white; my feet were sinking deep into snow, and this made walking very slow. Time was working against me: The snowstorm was raging, and evening was approaching. The icy wind would have cut through even a sheepskin coat, and I was wearing only an old jacket. I was freezing—especially my hands. But not far ahead was a descent into the valley, where I thought I could find shelter from the wind. And so it was: On my left I saw a whole forest of dry thistle bushes left over from the summer. After twenty more paces—twenty times sinking into the snow, twenty times pulling my feet out—I understood that I was exhausted and that my feet were no longer obeying me. I brushed aside the snow under a thistle bush, and fortunately found a little shelter. Then I sat down on it and put my head on my knees, to shield my face from the wind. I immediately felt better. Wind and snow were raging above, but I was curled up in a ball and already not sensing the cold. Oh, how good this felt.

I woke up because someone was angrily shouting at me and yanking my shoulder. In front of me stood a short, hunchbacked old man. I had never met him before and would never meet him again. What was he doing in the empty steppe in this snowstorm? I could not make out his face; his hat, his mustache, and his collar, raised up to his ears, were all covered with snow. He kept shaking me and screaming for me to get up. "You must not sit down, you will freeze, you must go immediately, for it will be dark soon!" Strangely, he seemed to know me—several times, he waved his hand toward the vegetable-garden brigade.

"I will go," I said. "Don't you worry, I will get there. Thank you."

For the last time he waved his hand. And immediately vanished. In such snow gusts it only took two steps for one to disappear. I did not even notice in which direction he had gone.

I rose. Indeed, the darkness was approaching—two or three hours earlier than I expected. Had I slept that long? My headscarf and shoulders had whole snowdrifts on top of them. But that could have happened in minutes in such a furious storm. Strangely, I felt totally rested and warmed up, and walked now as if I had just closed the schoolhouse door behind me.

It was completely dark when I finally trudged up to the door of the vegetable-garden brigade. Our two windows were lit and smoke billowed from the chimney. I stood for about two minutes, leaning against the door, just to catch my breath. I guess I was tired after all.

Everybody screamed when I opened the door, and Mama dashed up to me and grabbed my hands. The stove was crackling with all its might, the broiler lamp was shining on the table, and everything was hot. Everybody was shaking me, dusting off the snow, helping untie my headscarf. I had then a completely new feeling of double happiness. I was happy that it was over, but also even happier that it had happened. I'd managed it after all. I'd walked to school—and I'd come home. So simple. But not so easy.

Later, in the spring and summer, I walked out of my way many times to that patch of thistle bushes. I kept hoping to see the old man. But I never saw anyone on that deserted stretch of road, far from any house.

Except once. It was Spring, and I was walking slowly home from school, tired from slogging through the mud on the road. Near the familiar spot, I saw a man walking not on the road, but straight across fields. Why? Out here, far from the village and its subdivisions, you only encountered locals who walked (or, more often, rode) somewhere on business, and who knew the road well. I realized that something was wrong with this man. He was walking gingerly, as if not knowing where he was, and now he came straight toward me.

The man didn't look young but maybe he seemed older because of his heavy beard and unkempt appearance. He greeted me, almost affectionately, but somehow not in a way that adults greet children. Strange.

"You got any bread, girl?" he asked. And suddenly smiled, quite incomprehensibly, perhaps in apology.

I had eaten my whole breakfast in school, but to make sure he didn't think I was greedy I opened my sack and showed him: only my schoolbooks.

"All right, then," he said (he didn't speak the local dialect very clearly). "You take care."

"Maybe you'll come to our hut?" I asked. "We have bread and potatoes at home. And milk."

He gave a start.

"No, no. I can't."

"It's close." I pointed. "Over there, in the vegetable-garden brigade."

He shook his head quickly and, as if suddenly in a hurry, waved and walked off into the steppe. He looked back twice, but did not stop.

I stood on the road for a long time. I was not little anymore (nine years old!) and understood everything. This was a deserter. Deserters were cowards and traitors. They betrayed their military duty to defend the Motherland from the Fascists to the last drop of blood. They were afraid to die. They should be tried and shot. And every honest person must hate and expose them.

I was confused, for I felt no hatred nor a desire to expose this man. How could I hate this hungry man when I knew so well what hunger was like? Was he a coward? Perhaps—he kept glancing around, as if afraid even of me. I disliked cowards. But I had already read Furmanov's *Chapayev* and had been stunned when Commissar Klychkov (Furmanov himself) lost his nerve in his first battle. I was even more surprised by the way other Red Army soldiers reacted: They simply pretended that they had seen nothing—they must have encountered this before. There was no great shame for Klychkov. And he later turned out to be a brave man. But what if everyone had hated him after that first battle? What if they had shot him? Mama said that this was a truthful episode with a valuable lesson: that a brave man is not he who feels no fear—there are almost no such people—but he who has enough character not to submit to his fear. She said that the Red Army soldiers had behaved wonderfully. She always noticed, when she worked in the countryside, that simple people have a great deal of tact and some special sensitivity. What a pity it is that other, not-so-simple people, often lack it . . .

But still, this deserter was a traitor—and I had invited him to our home without hesitation. What would Mama have said? Here I had not the slightest doubt: She would have sat him down at the table and fed him everything we had, and then packed him some more for the road. I had never heard her use the word "expose." Instead I heard "Try to understand." When

that man had visited us on his bicycle once, Yelizaveta Nikolayevna was suspicious after his departure. "Isn't it strange, a
young and able-bodied man not at the front? Why was he not
mobilized? Did he dodge the draft? Here in the steppe it is easier . . ." Then Mama, in a firm, stern voice she rarely used, ob-
jected. "These days many lives have become incomprehensible
to outsiders," she said, "and this is not these people's fault. Before expressing surprise or condemnation, one should try to understand what they have endured. Almost always, it will turn
out that they did not choose their destinies themselves." Yelizaveta Nikolayevna fell silent.

I memorized shreds of this conversation because of
Mama's unusual tone: *these days . . . incomprehensible lives . . . not their
fault . . . people did not choose their destinies . . .*

Standing in the middle of the steppe then, I was far from
understanding that I had already been presented with a choice
between two truths. I met a hungry, hounded, miserable man.
According to our family truth, whoever he was, he was to be
helped and fed. But according to a louder and more powerful
truth that came from newspapers, radio, and books, he was to
be hated and exposed. That truth did not care that he needed
a meal and probably had not slept under a roof in a long time.
Perhaps I would not have cared either if I had never been hungry or homeless. And if I had not lost touch with newspapers
and radio . . . Perhaps that's how our own home truth had
begun to take over my soul so confidently, shoving aside the
other truth. As I watched the man's back shrinking in the distance, I felt a deep shame that I would soon enter my warm hut

without him, and a bowl of hot golden corn chowder would be placed in front of me.

More than half a year had passed since Mama and I walked through this same steppe, perhaps on this very same road. We had slept on the grass under the poplars. Almost like him. But back then it was warm. And dry.

I trudged forward, still sorting everything out. And then something else hit me. For the first time, I had seen a man who was sentenced to death.

Back then, nothing was simpler or more natural than death. It was as ordinary as the flu is in normal times. Each of us could die at any minute—from hunger, bombs, bullets, cold, or fire. Death walked among us, and people fell by the dozens around us. But none of us was sentenced. Each of us could hope for a miracle, for survival. Not him. He had been condemned to die by people just like myself—they wrote his name on a piece of paper, and he would not escape. But why? Was he worse than others? But what about the party bosses in Mama's story who were fleeing Kuschevka with their feather beds? They did not take up guns and fight, as old men did in Leningrad's People's Brigades. Weren't they cowards too? Why could *they* run, with their things and their cars?

Gray waves of clouds were passing overhead, lower and heavier, and the chilling wind was blowing harder. The steppe had never appeared so sullen and inhospitable. It was as if it were a vast realm of hopelessness and exile for the man who walked off to where the clouds were merging into a thick black wall. Sentenced to death.

SCHOOL CAME TO AN END, and I was very sad. Even the wonders of the spring and summer steppe could not replace it for me.

True, life was becoming more stable and reliable. We had located Father, he was alive! Our attestation resumed, and there was no more hunger. But even before that, the collective farm's administration had offered Mama a job as a land surveyor. She agreed without hesitation. This was very hard work. From morning until evening she had to circle the fields of the vegetable-garden brigade, measuring the acreage sowed, weeded out, or harvested during the day with two wooden sticks. She had to record what was planted, how many people worked on it, and for how many hours. This had to be done every day. When the sun baked the clay soil until it was covered with a cracked crust, or when rain made walking through the field a near-torture (after every three or four steps, the soles of your shoes would be weighed down with glue-like mud), Mama would come home tired, soaked by the rain or blackened by the sun. Then she had to spend long evening hours with her audit books, compiling reports about acreage planted, staffing of brigade teams, and man-hours worked. She had no real days off; there is no such thing in the fields. But she was still genuinely happy to have a job, an opportunity to be with people, and to be "in business," as she liked to put it.

When the steady spring heat set in, our life changed a great deal. Nights grew increasingly hotter. As field work often lasted from dawn to dusk, it was not uncommon for someone from the brigade to be forced to stay overnight in our hut. Mama, of course, found a solution.

We had a little stable in the yard, occupied for the whole winter by Aunt Khvenya's cow and the two farm horses—a black hot-tempered Spunky and another one, my favorite, whom I called Honey. She was amazingly tender. Spunky would rip bread out of my hands, shaking her head and wheezing, as if to say, "Don't think you're doing me any favor." Honey would patiently lower her head (I was very short, having completely stopped growing during these hungry years) and would unhurriedly chew the bread around my fingers, carefully touching them with her soft lips.

When I started learning to ride her, her careful friendliness had no limits. The hardest part was to get back up on Honey after we'd ridden to the river, in the middle of the steppe, without a saddle or stirrups, with only an old bridle. There was not even a hint of a tree stump or big rock here, and each time new contortions had to be invented. Honey would always understand everything and look at me with compassion, figuring out from one word what I wanted: I would, of course, talk to her, while she understandingly looked at me and nodded her big head to signal either accord or encouragement. She would stand, unflinching, at the bottom of the river bank while I climbed to the top of it and then slowly, so as not to hurt her, slid down on her back. And then it was enough to lightly touch her with my bare foot or slap her neck, and she would know which road to take or when to pick up the pace. Not a single cloud ever crossed our friendship.

By summertime, the cow and both horses were transferred from the stable into the yard, under an awning. They had buckets with food and water outside, and the stable would remain empty until well into autumn. That's when Mama started a project that sparked unanimous scorn from both Yelizaveta Nikolayevna and Aunt Khvenya, who rarely agreed on anything. She declared that she could easily sleep in the stable. She cleaned it thoroughly, washing it several times and scrubbing the floor with sand, airing it out for long periods each time. And then Mama started bringing in heaps of sweet-smelling herbs from the steppe. First she covered the entire floor with a layer so dense that the floorboards were not only invisible but couldn't even be felt under this soft aromatic carpet. Then she brought in heaps of flowers. In the meantime our whole colony of children got involved in the game, competing with each other to find anything rare or beautiful that grew in the steppe. Mama wove wreaths, garlands, and things resembling nets—she was a master at this—and the stable walls, just like the floor, were soon covered with astonishing rugs. Even from the ceiling hung batches of absinthe and feather-grass. In the corner we put a wooden trestle-bed with a fresh hay cover—this was where she slept. And on the windowsill, covered with an embroidered towel, stood books and a bouquet of flowers in a clay jug. Of course, everything was constantly renewed, since the flowers and herbs would quickly fade and dry up.

Adults disapproved, but we children adored the place. It was amazing and unusual. As soon as you opened the door, you would be overcome by a fresh cool wave, saturated with the strongest scents of the steppe. There was something magical about all the wreaths and bunches and the very smell of the steppe, locked and hiding in this green twilight, as if it had been tamed and had settled down here for a long time.

It was also a stunning discovery that so much unexpected beauty could be created from completely ordinary things, things we saw all around ourselves, which had always seemed modest in nature. Here they remained themselves yet were also transformed.

Even farm women, when they stopped by the brigade, would call each other over to "go look in on what Leksandrovna has put together." They would stand at the threshold, shaking their heads, so many things showing on their faces. There was a shade of confusion at this city woman's eccentricity, some surprise at the amount of effort required, appreciation (they knew how to value work), and also doubt (was it worth it?). And always somewhat involuntary approval. "Very pretty," they whispered. But there was also a certain feminine compassion, which I only understood later. It came from the knowledge that behind this was simply a young woman's nostalgia for her own home.

But no matter how much I loved the stable, I still slept in the hut. I had a secret reason for this. Left alone in our half of the room, I could now stay up late with a broiler lamp and a book. Everyone on Yelizaveta Nikolayevna's side went to bed early and slept soundly, so my lamp bothered nobody. Meanwhile, Mama was suffering from insomnia and tormenting migraines out in the stable. Back then, I had no appreciation for what her insomnia must have been like after all that we had lived through.

Now I was spending my whole days in the fields or in the steppe. It became my passion in the spring sowing season. Sitting in the grass, I never got tired of watching the unhurried transformation of the land. A silent empty field would suddenly be covered by even furrows. Then an old seed drill, to which our Spunky was harnessed, would swing like a pendulum from one end of the field to the other. On top of it sat Mikola Danilenko—our best friend. He was sixteen years old, still two years short of the draft. Until then, just like all boys his age, he'd served as a replacement for the men who went to the front. He was appointed a stableman for our vegetable-garden brigade, and from morning until evening he was busy with the horses. Quite often he would sleep over at our hut, and was a frequent guest at our evening readings, which we had resumed. We considered him one of us. He was a special favorite of Mama's, and he was the one to sit me on top of a horse for the very first time. If something didn't work out for me, he would make fun of me pitilessly, and I would respond in kind.

Once Mikola had done his work, a leveled-up furrow seemed to sigh with satisfaction. It had a completely different appearance from the fallow soil two steps away, across the divider, as if it already knew that within a week it would be covered with thick, even growth, and a little later it would completely disappear beneath green leaves.

And then would come a time when the field was a challenge to cross. If it was a cornfield, it would stand with its thin long leaves spread gallantly like a fancy dress, and from the tight envelopes of the stems bright locks of shiny blond hair would emerge. If it was a field of sunflowers, it would turn into a dense crowd of amusing tall creatures with bright yellow wreaths around their heads. There was something touching about the patient devotion with which they worshipped the sun, with never a break. I knew in advance at what hour they would face the road, and when they would turn their backs. I liked wiggling into the middle of their crowd, touching their fuzzy-haired leaves, looking into their faces, and inhaling their honey smell.

But time went on, and something unexpected and incomprehensible began happening to me, dimming all the pleasures of my summer steppe.

All that had happened to us in besieged Leningrad, on the "Road of Life," during our endless trip south on the train, and in the first months of our life in Kuschevka—all this had seemed hidden somehow, as if it hadn't happened to me. I did not cry, did not grieve, did not fear, and did not complain. It was as if I was frozen inside a glacier. Perhaps I simply had no strength to respond to what was happening around me. So some device in my consciousness was recording, precisely and without sentiment, every word, movement, and scene, filing them away in an invisible corner. And I, in complete passivity, was simply present during these events, nothing more.

But when I had slowly healed, and my strength gradually returned, something stirred in that dark corner. The day Dagmara and I visited those Leningrad women, it happened for the first time; a stunningly accurate recollection of our railcar. These were quiet and surreptitious tremors: Suddenly one picture or another would come back. Just our Leningrad apartment, darkened against German bombers—its big windows, covered from top to bottom with black fabric, so that no thin slice of light escaped outside. A broiler lamp sits on the table, and we are all crouched around the tiny portable metal stove, whose chimney pipes into our unused huge Dutch fireplace. We are drying our food ration for the day on the chimney pipe—minuscule slices of bread, "eighths." We look at them and cannot tear our eyes away, we cannot think of anything else.

Or suddenly I would see the entrance to our apartment building, the front door on Lesnoy Avenue. Every day Mama sent me and Vadik outside to walk just a little bit, saying that some fresh air was as good as an extra slice of bread. For several days a frozen corpse lay outside. Maybe it was one of our neighbors; he lay facedown and we could not see who he was. We would step over the corpse with difficulty, as it lay across the entrance and blocked our way. We were constantly encountering corpses. They were dragged off on sleighs while we walked—without coffins, of course, just wrapped in sheets. Sometimes a frozen figure would be still standing, leaning against the wall. No face could be seen behind the headscarf and coat collar. Was it a person who had stopped, feeling weak? Or someone already dead? Nobody knew.

Once Mama returned from the store shaken up. She'd seen a truck loaded with uncovered bodies, piled up in rows like logs. We had heard that such trucks circled Leningrad constantly, picking up frozen corpses, but none of us had seen one yet. One dead young woman's hair, Mama remembered, had come undone. And her loose, blond braid flapped against the side of the truck. And now I imagined that I myself was walking toward this truck and watching, among all these frozen bodies, the only living and moving thing—that loose blond braid.

And then I recalled how Vadik and I changed places in the bread line. This was at the former "Gastronom" on the first floor of our building on the corner of Lesnoy Avenue and Vyborgskaya Street. Vadik has a number written on his sleeve or back with chalk. He is leaving to go warm up at home. In a half-hour he would come back, and then I would go up to warm myself. Or I would remember how Mama brought water from the Neva River. Each day she would take the sleigh, on which Vadik and I had once ridden in the Nobel Gardens. (Was that really us? Riding on a sleigh?) She would load onto it a bucket with a lid, a big boiling pan, and some milk-cans. Then she'd put on a ski suit, wrap a scarf around her head, and leave for a long time. It was so far—down Vyborgskaya Street, then Karl Marx Avenue, toward the Military Medical Academy, and then past its dormitories down to Neva itself. There, across the Academy, was an ice-hole. Mama would drag the icy sleigh home behind her. Then each item separately—the bucket, the cans, the pan, and the sleigh itself—had to be brought upstairs to us on the third floor. Walk up. Then back down. Walk up again. And again, down.

Or I would remember how, when I took some fat book off a shelf, I suddenly saw behind it a little red box of chocolates we had eaten before the war (the lid had a picture of a running golden deer on it). I opened it, then almost dropped it. It was full of tiny pieces of bread—dry uneaten crusts, crumbs, and even a tiny piece of sugar. How, from where? This shelf belonged to me and Vadik, nobody else ever touched it, it stood in an empty frozen room. Stunned, I brought the box to Mama. For some reason it scared her and she stared at the box for a long time, not touching the pieces. Then I got scared too. How could Vadik, who suffered hunger more than anybody and was melting before our eyes, be able to leave something aside from his miserable eighth? That's when a neighbor came by to visit us. Mama started telling her about the box, and she seemed to understand immediately. She began nodding her head, "This means he'll die soon," she said calmly. And now I, after a year and a half, could hear plainly next to me this level, tired voice. "This means he'll die soon."

At first these visions would come and go. Then they would return again. Then more and more, dozens, hundreds of pictures and voices. Each time I saw them more lucidly. Each detail would freeze and repeat itself until it sunk its claws into my memory—and then I could not tear myself away. Gradually this became a torturous nightmare, as if a horde of bats flapped at me from all sides, viciously, persistently, and mercilessly. At times I could almost not see or hear the people around me. I would only see our dark room with black windows, see Tanya in Mama's arms or Vadik covered with a blanket on the medics' stretcher.

And most terrible was that suddenly, an awareness of the horror of all that had happened to us awoke inside me. It was as if everyone had died not a year ago, but only today. And only now did I realize that I would never see Vadik, Tanya, or Grandma again, that my whole life would now be without them—not a life but a stump of a life, forever without them. The realizations of death and despair gradually took root inside me, tearing into me whenever they wanted, and I was helpless. I would sit in the shadows near our hut with a book. And suddenly I would begin seeing through it—a live Grandma, smiling and grinding freshly washed potato skins, Tanya sitting nearby and staring at the pot. "Today we will bake some crepes . . ." I would jump up and run away into the steppe. There I would fall facedown on the ground and suffocate with convulsive sobbing. With all my strength I would press my eyes and mouth to the dry hot soil, to the prickly stems, trying to choke this memory, these voices. But nothing helped. And I would cry until I was completely exhausted.

There was nowhere to hide. Books offered no shelter, there were traps inside them at every turn—occasional mentions of death, an illustration with the body of a dead hero. "Orina, A Soldier's Mother" became intolerable for me, yet against my will I knew it by heart. The greatest torture was these plaintive moans:

> For nine days Ivan was sick,
> On the tenth day he croaked.

Reading again my favorite Cervantes, I would suddenly open to the page where Don Quixote descends into the Montesinos cave to talk to the dead king—and across from it was a print by Doré, and to this day I can picture the net of pale lines under which everything seems unreal and dead. Don Quixote stands there, his head bowed, and the revived king is rising from his coffin. And now there was no more Doré or Cervantes, but everything around me was being covered with the same pale veil, and I no longer felt myself in the living world.

Death was everywhere. And how could I live with the knowledge that somewhere nearby was a black abyss, which noiselessly grabs so many people from our world, one by one? As many as it wants, whenever it wants. That's how it swallowed Vadik, Grandma, and Tanya—they were standing next to me, then suddenly fell into it. Why did it bypass me? I was the weakest, sick during my entire childhood, not a single children's disease passed me by. So it must be coming back for me. When will it happen, and how? What will happen when I too collapse into it? They were all buried in the earth. But for me the land could not have anything at all to do with this deep abyss. I know, I know it is somewhere near, very near. Right now it is gaping behind my back. I cannot see it, but it sees me. What has it decided about me? Should I turn around? Here, I have turned around, and still do not see it. But it is here. It will appear only when it decides that it is my time too.

The most awful time was night, when I was locked inside four walls, full silence all around me and nothing to occupy my eyes and ears. I would sit up on the bed. The darkness watched me with the eyes of the dead, speaking and stirring. I would hope to wait it out, but each minute only grew worse. Finally, almost in a delirium, losing my grip on what is and what seems, I would jump up and run across the yard to Mama's stable.

Poor Mama did not know what to do with me. She was working from dawn to dusk, sleeping poorly, tormented by her own insomnia, and I would not let her rest even at night. But what could I do, where could I go with my misery? She would caress me, console me, and calm me down with those words that only mothers know. Sitting near her on the bed, I would gradually recover; a safe zone existed around Mama. She would patiently and tenderly talk me out of it. She would promise that during the holiday we would go to the village together, to the bazaar, and buy some gift for me there. And these uncomplicated promises and thoughts about a noisy bazaar would somehow return me to the real world.

"This will pass, Lenochka, it will pass," she said. "The same things happen to me. We have to live through it and persevere. We survived a horrible time, and it cannot go away just like that, but you have to live and cope . . ."

Mama wanted to return to the hut, but I would not agree. I liked being able to run away somewhere. Then, halfway calmed, I would leave her and stop by the yard. The night was also kind to me, the fresh air made it easier to breathe. The high, wide sky glowed at me with all its constellations, hazes, and the Milky Way. Under the awning nearby lay Honey and Spunky, snoring loudly in their sleep. Such a good smell of fresh hay and hot horse breath came from there. The fullness and quiet of this life would slowly invade me and wash away the dark spill on my tormented conscience. Here, out in the dark, I had no fears at all. I would walk around the yard, my shadow pacing ahead of me in the moonlight, deliberately and calmly, as if it just came out for a stroll from a muggy hut. Nowhere will one find such clear, strong, and deep sleep as in a windless night steppe. The whole earth closes its eyes, the grass stands still, the tired road straightens out, and you can no longer resist and continue, among this unlimited sleep, with your own restless life. I would quietly return to the hut, lay down, and fall asleep.

†

THIS LASTED for a long time, and could have probably grown into some serious chronic illness, if not for Mama. She was anxiously monitoring me, trying to foresee my fits in advance. Sometimes they did not happen for two or three days. I was just like everyone else, running around, singing songs, going to the Yeia for a swim, taking horses out to pasture, and reading. And then suddenly I would stop eating, avoid people, try to quietly sneak out to the steppe—nobody knew where to find me or when I would return. I would come back disheveled, exhausted, reclusive, and crawl into a corner somewhere. I would not respond to questions, would not explain anything, and could insult someone whose attention became overbearing. I would stay there until Mama returned from work. With her around I would thaw a bit and try to contain myself.

Finally Mama began subtly interfering in my feverish life, carefully diverting it into other channels. She tried for a while to distract me from books. At first she just tried screening them very carefully, but soon became convinced that screening was no guard against anything. A fit might be triggered by *The Last of the Mohicans,* by Gogol's *Terrible Revenge,* or by any volume of poetry. Even Pushkin with his "Song About the Clairvoyant Oleg" was dangerous, and one could forget about Lermontov:

And suddenly then from the coffin
An awakened emperor rises.

Mama disliked prohibitions, and would not condone them, especially with me. She was right. An outright prohibition of reading (and she could have simply stopped bringing me books from the Churakovs) would only have aroused "the spirit of opposition" in me, as she called it. But in careful and crafty ways she would try to occupy me with something else. During the time she was not working, Mama would always be near me. In the evenings she would often lead us in singing. This was our favorite pastime now, replacing our winter reading. When it would get dark and the air more brisk, we would carry benches out of the hut and put them by the door. There we would all sit and sing for two or three hours, until supper.

It is amazing how much people used to sing then, being tired and having endured so much. How they needed it! Old farmer women who visited us for lunch break—to rest up from the afternoon heat and to have a "salty snack" with a slice of bread, a tomato, a cucumber, and a piece of lard—would neatly shake the crumbs off their skirts, fix their headscarves, and start up a collective drawling song as they sat in the shade. We soon knew all their songs by heart and sang along with them. Often they'd ask us to sing some of our songs; they liked the long story-ballads the most. They could sit motionless for a long time and listen to "Raging Storm, Noisy Rain," "Our Proud 'Viking' Would Not Surrender," "How Moscow Burned," or at least "No Town Noises Can Be Heard" and "Near Muromskaya Road Stood Three Pine Trees." It must have looked strange: Leningrad women and children sitting under the bushes among stern and concentrating Cossack women, and above us distant shadows floating: Yermak, deeply pensive on the coast of the Irtysh River; Napoleon, standing with his arms crossed on his chest near a Kremlin window; sailors on the deck of a burning ship; or a young man imprisoned in a dark castle.

We had long since befriended our brigade women. Mama was particularly happy with this friendship now, because it was easier to force me to be among people. Under different pretexts—to help with something, to deliver something, or sometimes without any excuse—she would send me off to the field with one team or another. Many walked, carrying weeding tools on our shoulders, but sometimes I rode in a cart that was headed in the same direction. And there, among general mayhem, constant joking, chewing of seeds, and cursing of the stubborn ox, I would completely forget my horde of bats.

In the field I would see Mama from afar, walking down a divider with her two-footed measuring device, which under her hands was pacing across the field like a crane. Once when I spotted her, I suddenly remembered that before the war Mama used to be a sports fanatic. She liked shooting, but was above all a crazy bicyclist, and even several accidents did not cure her of that passion. She was holding the measuring stick just like she once held a bicycle's handlebars. Or she would be sitting in the grass, writing measurements in her journal with great concentration. Here in the field, Mama seemed different and unusual. She was friendly with everyone, as always, and when women entangled her in their joking contests that ran across the entire field, she would join and yield no ground to anyone. But when she was deeply engrossed in her measurements and calculations, everyone left her alone with respect. I could see that she enjoyed considerable stature despite all her simplicity.

Mama had a lucky skill of finding a common language with very different kinds of people. It was because of her youth, she would explain, teaching in remote village schools. But judging from her own stories, even in her childhood she was drawn out of the house, attracted to people—to listen, to socialize, and to befriend. When a Gypsy tribe would come into town, she was the first to run over to visit their camp, and sing around the campfire as if she were one of their own.

Sometimes a particularly old cart would squeak down the road, raising huge clouds of dust, and everyone would know it was the brigade manager, Nikifor Kondratich Artiukh. He had been sent home from the front with some serious injury. But he still wore his military shirt, bleached almost white by the sun and crisscrossed by a worn leather belt, as well as his cap, under which he was always drenched with sweat. Jumping off the cart, he would run across the furrows, stumbling and yelling— something had been done wrong in the field, or not done at all. And the women greeted him with instant resistance. Actually everybody liked him, but this was a deep-rooted unspoken Cossack rule: You cannot submit to authority; if you give in too much you will regret it later. And they cut him no slack. Unhurriedly, but in unison, a crowd of feisty Cossack women would surround him from the furrows. Quipping as they gathered, they would interrupt his stuttering speech with short acerbic remarks, and soon a communal chorus would begin. There was never a real quarrel, but the air would heat up with jabs and jokes, the chorus intensifying, as not a single person remained silent. Nikifor Kondratich was hardly in any shape to defend, much less attack, and his declarations could scarcely be heard through "the artillery," as he called it. Eventually, he would take off his cap, wipe his wet face with a dusty palm, and fall silent. This was capitulation, and it was greeted by thunderous, united laughter.

I was left alone so rarely that my fits were becoming rarer and weaker. There were always people around, most of all Mama. Between the two of us, sentimental tenderness and playfulness were not habitual. But every day, Mama would find a creative way to occupy me, or to make me happy, with something special. There were small gifts like a new notebook or a tiny pot with a handle. Once there was a story that something resembling a polecat was seen behind our barn. Then Nirs and I were off to guard her chickens, hunt for the polecat, search for its burrow—a whole arsenal of tricks was used. Mama and I both loved animals, and one day she came back from the steppe with an amazing, gorgeous gift—two rabbits, one white and one gray. I became inseparable from these warm fluffy creatures. They seemed quiet and mellow, but had a cunning and enterprising nature. They were forever chewing something, digging tunnels, and trying to escape. It was immediately necessary to make their housing arrangements, to find out what they preferred for food and bedding, and then run endless errands to the field or steppe to bring them this or that. I was constantly busy with their care.

One Sunday, Mama said she was going to the cemetery and asked if I wanted to come along. I was surprised and a bit scared, but still agreed to go. After we trimmed and weeded, cleaning up the two tiny, flower-covered hills at the very edge of the village cemetery as well as we could, we sat down together on the grass. Then Mama spoke. She said that she always felt easier here. That, maybe, the same will be true for me. If Vadik's grave had been here too, we would have all been together. Mama said that when they all died, her greatest anguish was that she had stopped believing in God during her childhood. Since she did not believe in the afterlife, she could not hope that we would meet them again. But there was an immortality in which she did believe. If we continued to grieve for them, it meant they did not cease to exist for us. We both suffered because we missed Grandma, who cared about all of us before herself until the last minute of her life; we missed Tanya, who was so cheerful and tender; and Vadik, so serious and kind. But since we remembered all this about them, they lived on in us. The fact that we remembered them and still loved them was their immortality.

Sometimes it got very hard for us. But there is one thing, my mother said, that lightened our lives. They did not get to live out theirs—and we owed a duty to them, since we lived on. She told me that I should remember more often: I am alive, and they are not. This, perhaps, would restrain me from doing things I might regret. Or, it might help me to do something difficult, which I otherwise would not have resolved to do. I must always simply think: I am alive, and they are not. They can no longer do anything, but I can. And thus it will be as if they participate in our lives, and live through us.

We suffered a great deal of grief, but we were not alone. Nearly every family and every person has suffered. There were still the two of us left, and one day Father would be with us.

Others had no one, and nothing to hope for. I should some-times try to remember this, she said, when I felt very bad. We cannot be overcome by our own grief, and only live in that grief. If everybody did that, people would become very selfish and indifferent. It's better for people to start helping each other—then there will be less grief for everybody. She asked me to consider this from time to time. When I felt like running away to cry, maybe it would be better to look around and try to make sure that somebody next to me doesn't start crying. I would feel better myself when I acted this way.

Mama had never spoken to me like this before, as if I were already grown up. She was not consoling or pitying, as before. More than a year ago when I fell exhausted at the threshold of a hut, she picked me up and carried me across it. Now, across this new threshold, I had to walk myself. Everything inside me rose up and clashed in confusion. I was afraid of losing my shield, my Mama who always stood between me and my prob-lems. But another sense also grew from those same roots. I was now regarded as an adult, expected to do something more than study my homework well or keep my hands clean. I had to summon some force within, which would help me defeat my dark plague. I had to take this step on my own.

It was akin to my feeling on that stormy winter afternoon, when I stepped out the door of my school. Why, without a doubt, had I decided that I must go? Some internal clock told me: It's time, you have to. You cannot stay inside the warm school—you will miss something important. Now Mama re-minded me about that clock, its hands again approaching some important point. But Mama just showed me the hands, and it was up to me to do the right thing.

I was not aware that all this unease inside me was simply a first step toward exiting from childhood into the outside world.

We returned to the hut. I never again had a single fit as terrible as the ones I had had before. Sometimes they would approach, but I would manage to choke them back. It was not easy. My grief and despair did not go away in one day, or one month, but it became different. Without the desperate explosions which were eroding my will to live, I was healing. Slowly, it seemed, but soundly.

Summer itself was helping. Our winter life in the hut had been reclusive and lonely, but now we became unrecognizably lively and noisy. It was as if we were transported all at once from total abandonment into a busy town center, where from dawn to dusk there was no end to conversations, shouts, slamming doors, laughter, and singing. There was the banging of repair work in the yard, and splashing water by the well, where the bucket rang all day. Some were washing up after the dusty road, others stopped by for a sip, and Aunt Khvenya was doing the laundry. She covered the yard with her shirts, skirts, towels, and sheets, astonishing me with her wealth.

I liked wandering in the steppe, far from home. Having reached a place where neither a hut nor a tree could be seen, I would lie down on my back in the grass, and look up. Everything was simple, generous, and immense—just what I needed. It was quiet and endless: fields with rye, virgin lands with feather-grass, unpopulated roads, and a huge clear sky. Time flowed slowly and widely. Here there was no clock, just the sun and the horizon. The wind didn't really blow in summer, it only breathed long titanic breaths, which would barely bend the grass above my face. These slow waves would pass right above me. And with each one, some of the corrosive darkness inside me would be diluted and washed away toward the hills, while something pure and firm flowed in and remained in its place. It was becoming easier and easier to breathe.

Some days I would stay close, sitting near the well in our yard, in the shadow of the bushes, with a book in my hands. Reading went especially smoothly there. As I later understood, Mark Twain's books about the Mississippi, James Fenimore Cooper's books about forests, and Jules Verne's book about sea islands are not meant to be read within four walls. One must sit down on the grass with these books, so that an acacia's shadow jogs across the pages, so that the wind stubbornly rustles its leaves and your pages. Next to me on the grass, overripe berries from a mulberry tree were falling, a dragonfly circling above them. It was a strange and happy feeling, rocking on the waves of a stream that flowed from one world into another: a trail through a dense grove—the smell of a rye field across the road—a night bonfire on a riverbank near a fort—the monotonous pacing of oxen on the road—the sails filling with wind, and the deck tilting now under a growing northeast breeze.

Sometimes though, into this stream, would suddenly flow something alien to both these worlds—memories of Leningrad. After the wave of euphoria upon the arrival of our troops subsided, people talked about Leningrad less and less often. It was too obvious that going back would be difficult. But we couldn't keep it out of our thoughts. Only in Leningrad did we have a home. I could not stop dreaming about our library. "There you will finally be able to study for real!" Mama would say, and I would remember the imposing yet glamorous school on Vyborgskaya Street.

But I almost did not remember prewar Leningrad. We had moved there from Moscow, where I was born, less than two years before the war. I was very sickly in the unkind climate, spending far too many days inside our semi-dark rooms, which faced out onto a narrow yard. My associations of a happy and peaceful life among a big family were all from Moscow. I could picture so clearly the shadowy parks of Sokolniki where we lived, with the bright sky and water of the Himki reservoir where we went to bathe with our friends and neighbors. The Moscow of my memories sprawled lightly, cheerfully, and freely, while Leningrad towered with gloom and reclusiveness. I was drawn to it, but I felt no closeness. And despite all my family had endured there, it did not truly feel like my home. It did not resemble the legendary St. Petersburg of Pushkin, which I already held within my heart: "Neva's stately flow, the granite on her shores." These two cities could not merge in my mind. I could not imagine my Leningrad future at all.

So I was all the more firmly attached to my present in the steppe. It was a place I felt I knew, with a child's sense of every bend and turn. But it was so bottomless, that every day brought something new and unexpected. The heat arrived, and in that valley where I had sat under the thistle bushes, the creek had almost dried up. Near the spring that was its source, the soil was no longer soft and cool, but had become hard as a rock.

The harvest in the cornfields was beginning. We children would go around with sacks and bags, picking up the remaining ears. Years later at an exhibit from the Louvre, I was stunned by the sight of Millet's *The Gleaners*. There in a Hermitage gallery I encountered something completely unforgotten, just below the surface awaiting its return: the sensation of the steppe's hot air in my face and prickly broken stems under my bare feet.

Not far from our hut was a small threshing floor. It attracted me like a magnet. I don't know if it was because of the Blockade hunger, but I had an almost religious regard for bread. This enormous mountain of fresh grain, glowing in the sun, evoked a special agitation in me. I would sit down at its base, or kneel there. Then I would slide my bare hands deep into the pile, a dry silky stream of grain flowing between my fingers. This mountain would breathe warmth on me, with its precious smell of sun and earth.

Later I would often try to convince my university professors that only by some misunderstanding, by some wind that got derailed from its track, I was blown into studying art history, and that I really was supposed to sow wheat, herd horses, and plant trees. They would laugh, but this wasn't entirely a joke.

Still, these happy hours in the fields were only a ray in the dark. Inside me remained a steady fear of the return of the nightmares, the bats. Dipping my palms into a grain hill, as if drawing water from a river, I was borrowing strength from the earth and its bounty. I could feel that everything around me was full of this healthy, firm strength—a strength that only flowed past me, but rarely into me. Until one day.

Our most important days stand apart from the calendar and even from outside events. So I have no idea what day it was, or rather evening, that my sea change came. It was sometime in the middle of the summer of 1943. Even the evening was nearing its end. Mama had gone to her stable, Yelizaveta Nikolayevna and Dagmara were fidgeting with their beds behind the stove, and I sat by the broiler lamp with a book. My favorite two hours were approaching—alone with a book and the broiler lamp. Then suddenly Mama reappeared in the doorway.

"Something incredible is going on in the steppe, it is simply impossible to go to sleep. You must all come out and walk down the road to see for yourselves. Such things cannot be missed, let's go!"

Dagmara and Nirs were instantly excited. If sleep in the muggy hut was being postponed, they were ready to walk as long as need be. But for me, my reading was being postponed, and I felt no happiness at all. Neither did Yelizaveta Nikolayevna.

"Galina Aleksandrovna, why this night excursion? Don't we see enough of the steppe during the day? We get so tired during the day, and you have a job too, I don't understand why you need this."

"As soon as we leave the yard you will understand. It's not just a night, it's a holiday. You will see, all your fatigue will be gone in a flash, and that alone merits the walk."

Eventually we all went, me last, slowly and unwillingly extinguishing the lamp. We left the yard, leaving behind the stable, the barns, and the high stack of fresh hay until there was nothing, except the sky and the steppe.

That's when something started changing, around and within me. It had always seemed that I knew the steppe by heart. In some sense this was true: I knew the herbs, trails, descents to the river, valleys, lizards, snakes, and birds, every field and divide. But now all these familiar things were invisible, and in the diffuse light of the stars, the Milky Way revealed itself with a breadth and clarity that powerfully drowned out the endless minutiae of my daily world.

For the first time I heard the night steppe. Wandering around the yard in the dark during my previous insomnia, I had heard only the domestic life of the yard—Spunky and Honey, the cow, the little piglet, and Aunt Khvenya's chickens. I never knew how triumphantly and happily everything sings in the steppe at night. Who were they—grasshoppers, cicadas, frogs by the river, night birds in the reeds? Everything around was ringing and drawling. Every minute something changed in the choir—some voices would subside, others would enter. Loud splashes of sound perked up by the river. I, who had never heard the ocean, thought that broad waves were rising and falling around us.

That vastness, which I adored so much by day, was nothing compared to the endless night, when the sky with all its constellations opened above the steppe. Some were bright, others barely flickered, halfway erased by the distance, and it seemed that their intensity surged and receded with the tides of ringing sound that were rising from the steppe grass up to the very Milky Way.

Where did it come from—such freedom, such bliss? The steppe was scarred all around by the war that had just passed over it. I knew where bomb craters gaped like round black lesions, which field was covered with shrapnel like pimples, and where the skin of the land had been shredded by tanks. Yet here it was, overflowing with nocturnal joy.

And we ourselves, having dipped into this all-drowning happiness, were no longer our former selves. We were not destitute homeless people, awaiting execution, under-eating today to save at least a slice of bread for tomorrow. We walked down this road lightly and happily, toward some promise, some expectation that we still had something left ahead. From our cramped and meager life, which fit into a tiny circle of light from the broiler lamp, we had suddenly stepped into this deeply and fully breathing world, so generous to us that one could not avoid believing, walking down this road, that there were no incurable wounds or unfullfillable dreams.

And I was no longer that yesterday self—a half-alive creature, apathetic, unable to grasp life, the helpless prey of bats. I walked down the soft and warm road on the firm bare feet of a village girl, who knew how to ride horses and walk across the steppe, no matter what the distance or weather. In this spaciousness, I seemed to grow. Something was painlessly subsiding, and something was flickering up ahead. Why all this came over me on that nameless, dateless night, I do not know. But for many years later, I drank from this memory as if from a river. It was a passage, my first and most important one.

❧

ONLY AFTER THAT NIGHT did I truly come back to life. An awareness that I was really living, that I was healthy and strong, filled me to the brim. On the outside, my life did not really change at all. But all colors became fresher and brighter, everything breathing more strongly and intensely than before. And every sound—feisty voices calling across the fields, Spunky and Honey neighing to greet me, the wind tearing straw from the roof before a thunderstorm—contained some new intonation, as if it were now addressed directly to me.

An unstoppable passion awoke inside me, to revive this sharp feeling every minute and to test the durability of this very gift of life. Whenever we lit a bonfire, I would throw in a whole heap of dry bushes at once, daring the fire to engulf my hands and face. Bringing the horses in from pasture, riding Honey bareback, I would urge her—faster, faster! Come on! It was the constant thirst of a childish rationale: If I survived all that, nothing could happen to me now. The fire will not touch me, the ice will not cave in under me, and the horse will not throw me! Even standing on top of a new haystack, I could not simply descend. I had to hurl myself off so that my breath stopped, my heart raced, and the wind whistled in my ears.

Even when that streak of recklessness passed, for years I continued to have relapses. In Leningrad, where there were no horses, steppe fires, or cliffs, one of my girlfriends and I came up with quite a dangerous alternative—climbing around dilapidated postwar city rooftops. Of course, only roofs above at least five floors would count, the steeper the better, and best of all, if there were no guardrails at their edge. It was especially good in winter, when the roofs were covered with snowdrifts. As we climbed one such rooftop near the Nobel Houses, a layer of snow gave way under us, and we started sliding. Speeding toward the unguarded edge of a six-story precipice, I experienced the feeling of sheer physical terror for the first time. Just in time, we managed to jump onto a window ledge past which our little glacier was sliding.

It all could have ended badly. Such a wanton waste of energy and thirst for strong sensation will sooner or later dull the soul and distort one's feelings. Most importantly, such cavalier bravery allows a person to fool himself. And once fooled, he will be satisfied, never having realized true, mature courage. In his novel *The Master and Margarita*, Mikhail Bulgakov gives Pontius Pilate this first kind of courage, but deprives him of the second kind. And there is the fearless warrior, who fiercely smashes into enemy lines on his horse, but freezes when he imagines the face of Tiberius in front of him. It is a fear he can neither overcome nor forgive in himself. "Cowardice is the worst of all vices," Jesus says, and Pilate knows that it's about him.

These words were censored out of the published version of Bulgakov's novel, only appearing in underground editions. It was politically unacceptable, in the Soviet Union, to suggest that there might be some other sort of courage, aside from a soldier's courage.

MAMA WOULD LEAVE for the fields at dawn and would only return at the end of the day. Left to myself, I would grab a piece of bread or a boiled ear of corn and dash out into the steppe. From morning until night, I'd take horses to pasture if they weren't working in the field, hunt for snakes and lizards, and sneak into the reeds of the half-dry Yeia to search for river birds. Or I'd simply go somewhere far, to look at a valley of still-green tumbleweeds, or to reach an unfamiliar barrow. I'd sit down on a hilltop, next to an old rock which looked like a flat column sunk deep into the ground. What was on it? Remains of a sign engraved by somebody, or cracks and scars from centuries of winds and rains? And who made this barrow in the middle of the steppe? The Scythians?

I had no desire to go home before the sun began tilting towards the horizon. Some bothersome itch kept pushing me to go further and further. It seemed as if, with time, a distance had developed between me and that amazing night. As if it had not fully flung the door open for me, like it seemed back then, but only nudged it ajar. I kept waiting. When will it come, the whole thing? In all my steppe wanderings I kept hoping to stumble across something, to encounter something necessary. But day after day, week after week, I searched and found nothing. I returned later and later to the vegetable-garden brigade.

The only things that could hold me at home at least temporarily were books. No matter how tired Mama was, no matter what the weather, if she had a free day she would go to the Churakovs. But almost their entire library had already visited us. Some books—Jack London, Mark Twain, Jules Verne, Gogol, Pushkin's prose (I had learned the poetry by heart, so there was no need to read it again)—we had borrowed two or three times. "You will soon run out of things to read," Mama said. "What will you do then? Already, all you want are your steppe adventures." This was true, and I stood by the door, impatiently shuffling my bare sunburned feet, all covered with scrapes. Indeed, I could not bring myself to sit inside the hut. The walls and ceiling were simply too oppressive for me.

Imperceptibly, my steppe adventures, as Mama dubbed them, which arose from a happy feeling of freedom and safety, were becoming irrepressible and uncontrollable. It was as if I was carried somewhere against my will. There was some extremity in them, which with time, I began vaguely sensing myself. I came to realize that the steppe was no longer giving me the joy it had before. More often now I was running into the wilderness to suppress something strange inside myself, something completely incomprehensible, something never felt before. It was like an emptiness where something should exist. As if there were a door somewhere that I needed to open in order to understand everything. But so recently I had not needed anything, everything had been nice and simple. What had changed?

A new crisis was looming.

It was resolved suddenly, though who could know that its very resolution would tie a new knot, this time for decades to come?

The number of the Churakovs' unread books was indeed dwindling. But, as usual, new friends were finding Mama themselves. She was asking everybody about books. And one day she returned home with the news that she had visited Yekaterina Ivanovna.

"She sent a book for you to read." Mama looked at me with doubt. "I took it, of course, but I don't know . . . "

And she pulled a fat, heavy leather-bound volume out of her bag, very ancient-looking—even I had never seen such a valuable book. It was inscribed with golden letters: "N. N. GNEDICH. GLOBAL HISTORY OF THE ARTS."

I reached out with distrust and not much interest. Probably something scholarly and boring. Really, why did I need this? For hundreds of pages nothing was happening, nobody was crawling through virgin forests or solving mysteries. The dense text was interspersed with illustrations, sometimes glued-in colored inserts, sometimes small drawings. "The Parthenon,"

"Alhambra," "The Paris Notre Dame Cathedral." For some reason the buildings surprised me even more than the ladies wearing tall caps with long veils or the servant boys in strange shoes with pointed toes.

"I'll look at it," I promised tersely.

In the evening after supper, during my usual reading time, I peeked at it several times, reading some random passage or looking at the pictures. Nothing was especially interesting. But when I was going to bed, and everything that had happened during the day was beginning to blur and melt away, through my mind there suddenly walked, slowly and clearly, a row of beautiful women. They walked with a light and proud gait, looking straight ahead dispassionately. Their white robes were streaming in folds, from their shoulders down to the marble blocks on which they walked. Our clay floor gleamed magically under the marble blocks, and the folded robes nearly brushed against me. I wished desperately that just one of them would turn around and look at me. But not a single one did. And so they left, silently, their gazes frozen on something that remained invisible to me. "The Acropolis of Athens," said a small voice in my mind. But I was already dreaming, a deep and unrepentantly happy dream.

Within several days I was inseparable from my new discovery. May God bless these ancient volumes with their ponderous text and primitive illustrations, which stood for decades on bookshelves in the most remote towns and steppe farmsteads. History marched on—revolution, civil war, collectivization, famine, destruction, another war—yet they firmly stood on their shelves, as if they knew in advance that their day would come again. "Gilded paint will fade away, but the pigskin will remain," they too were repeating the naïve and brilliant refrain from my favorite tale by Andersen. And the leather of their binding indeed remained, even the proud golden letters remained: *Global History of the Arts.* So generation after generation, like myself, could discover with surprise that somewhere in Rome Trajan's Column still stands, and the marble Ariadne is still sleeping credulously with her hand under her head, not knowing that the sails of Theseus' ships are already far at sea, and the wings of the Versailles Palace are still just as vastly spread underneath a towering clear sky.

Even before, I had not felt alone in the steppe. Now, however, not only was it populated with people close to me but above my head sprawled the Mauritanian arches of the Alhambra, and where I had previously seen only a vulture, patiently circling above, now the Gothic spires of Reims or Chartres trailed off into the clouds. And the steppe did not pale at all in comparison to these new wonders. On the contrary! Only then did I notice that a thistle leaf is just as patterned and pretty as the curls of acanthus on a Corinthian column. I noticed that the Cossack women we knew resembled the Amazons in their faces, postures, and even some of their clothing. I knew the countries of the world and saw that the abandoned railroad went from north to south. North was Leningrad. And South was the Alhambra, Rome, and Athens.

But why did I care about the Alhambra? Why in my thoughts was I walking around the Lions' Court, again and again? What was I finding there that was lacking in my steppe? Its marble, its opulence? But I was indifferent to this; our poverty never oppressed me. If sometimes I felt nostalgic for Leningrad, it was only because there, somewhere, perhaps, our rooms and books still remained, and there we would be living under our own roof.

Then what? It was beautiful? And what does beautiful mean, and why am I not indifferent to whether or not something is beautiful?

Even Mama was puzzled by my sudden passion for the *Global History of the Arts,* and my attempts to learn how to draw. I myself only found the explanation many years later when I read Dostoyevsky's saying: "Beauty will save the world." To my amazement, I found the key in these words. Unaware of it myself, I had behaved like a small, wounded animal, who through either an innate, thousand-year-old instinct or its mother's teachings finds among a multitude of plants the only one that will cure its wound—and, having found it, becomes inseparable from it.

And so it was. By some miracle I had survived, and even remained healthy. But this miracle was insufficient for the soul. Everything inside me had been uprooted by this life side-by-side with death, month after month, which even adults could not endure. Everything inside me had frozen during the horrible Blockade winter, when one thin slice of bread per day was our shield from everything: hunger, cold, darkness, shells and bombs, corpses and ruins on the streets. And the freezing of the soul. And then there was the hot, smoldering steppe, coffins in the next room, a German pistol in the face, homelessness and defenselessness, and lists for executions. I could feel my soul shrinking, curling up as some force of self-preservation shielded me with immobility and apathy. I forgot how to feel fear, I forgot how to suffer hunger. But this was not normal. And when strength returned to me, into this void burst a whole flood of feverish suffering, the belated horror of death.

Mama had done everything she could to guide me out of this dead end, to show me where I could find a ray of light. But that was her lesson, that I must do the main work myself. I tried as hard as I could. And after that amazing starry night, I felt completely healthy, strong, and happy. The strength stayed with me, but I could not hang on to happiness. I had regained my health, but for what? What next?

By the time they are ten years old, children have built their own world around themselves, one just as durable and defined as the walls of the house in which they live. I had neither my own home nor my own walls. We had no relatives. As for the ones who lived far away, we had long heard nothing or almost nothing from them. I had no friends my age and neither did Mama. We lived without strong human ties. We lived temporarily in every respect, our lifestyle had nothing reliable or solid. And no matter how generously the starry sky spread out above me, or how strongly the beauty of the steppe beckoned me to wander, stare, and be surprised, I was still living among ruins. With what was I supposed to build my world?

When I was visited in my dream by the women from the Acropolis, I wanted to find them again in Gnedich's book, then again and again. They did not turn to look at me. I saw them so briefly, but they left a deep mark. Why? Weren't my dreams crossed frequently by brave captains, gold diggers, even Neanderthals in animal skins who dreamed of precious fire? But they replaced one another too easily, even though I knew so much about each one and could see them all just as clearly. I knew nothing about these women in white, who walked by me without so much as a glance in my direction. And here I did not need to know. That was not the point.

I came back to the same questions. It was beautiful? And what does beautiful mean? Why am I not indifferent to whether or not something is beautiful?

When my ancient ancestors were building huts, somewhere between Pskov and Tver, why did they need to decorate their windows, roofs, and porches with delicate wooden carvings? This didn't make the hut warmer or more comfortable. My other ancestors, peasant women in Archangelsk villages, spent months of winter evenings sewing crosses into towels, weaving lace on bobbins, or embroidering holiday shirts with golden thread—why did they do that? Didn't they have enough worries with children and farming and housework?

Looking at the Alhambra's light arches—a ray of sunlight on marble, an opening into the neighboring court, a wall which stood in one's way with the puzzle of a strange writing, or a lion-fountain—I understood that this was all built by people who loved life and knew how to enjoy it. How pleasing this all was to the eye! For these people, everything was joy: sun, shade, marble, greenery, water, space, tiny corners, simplicity, and opulence. They gathered it all together and arranged it so that a person, walking behind them down the pathways they chose, would begin to see everything at its most beautiful, and would become just as happy as they were. With me, it happened every time.

I read everything about the Gothic style, but it was difficult and passed me by. I knew only that the people who built cathedrals in Chartres and Cologne were brave and free. "A town's air makes one free," that I understood well. When I looked at the tiny human figures above whom rows of columns so fearlessly and powerfully shot up into the sky, I always imagined the architect not among them, but somewhere outside, on top of an unfinished spire. He looked down on the little town, and wind was playing with his hair.

Then I would not have found proper words to even remotely describe what I was feeling. But my joy caused by the Alhambra's arches and palaces, and my soaring jubilation caused by Gothic cathedrals, were so strong that I relive them to this day.

I had no illusions that this special world I had discovered was free of misery and deprivation. I read about Mozart and Beethoven (although I had never heard their music, aside from what Mama sang—we had no radio). Mama told me a lot about Pushkin, his life and his places, and most important his poems. The words he wrote in exile in Mikhailovskoye, "Storm is shrouding sky with darkness," for me were about us, as if they were written for us.

Our sorry little hut
Is both sad and gloomy . . .

. . . on top of my decrepit roof
Straw will start to stir with noise . . .

That was the straw roof of our hut! How many times did I hear that noise in bad weather? He knew all that we lived with. And even when, to chase away the sorrow, he was asking his old nanny to "sing me a song, about how the blue tit-bird lived quietly overseas"—were these not our evening readings by the broiler lamp?

But this is what was astonishing to me. In that world, out of their own sadness and darkness, people could create something that would shine a bright light on someone else's sadness and darkness. This was the healing herb that I was groping for. I often looked up the statue of a wounded Amazon in Gnedich's book. She stood with her hand thrown behind her head, and her face turned upward with an expression both of pain and a sort of silent reproach. She was overpowering her pain. But why, in her countenance, was there no such despair as I felt? What did she know that I did not? Or perhaps her sculptor knew something? All I understood was that when I looked at her, I felt better and calmer.

The same thing would happen whenever I sat with Gnedich's book for a long time. As if a wounded Amazon woman or the spire of a Gothic cathedral were empowered to open for me such heights and expanses that my misfortunes began to seem less almighty and overwhelming. They would not become smaller or weaker—but I myself would become stronger and firmer. Some power would intervene on my behalf.

Years later, when I thought about Gnedich's book again, I found one more answer. Perhaps the most difficult aspect of our life on the steppe was not the poverty or even the danger. Completely uprooted from our city and home, from our usual way of life, we were aliens and had no rights whatsoever. We lived in somebody else's home. We lit somebody else's stove. We took water from somebody else's well with somebody else's bucket. After washing her metal milk cans, clay bowls and pots, shiny pans, and glass jugs, Aunt Khvenya would hang them upside down on fence poles. It was a vast assortment compared to our own sad collection. We had almost nothing between our family and Yelizaveta Nikoleyevna's. Even the land on which we walked was not our own. "Without you Commies we lived freely on our land," our first landlady's relative told me once.

But when I flipped through Gnedich's wonderful pictures, amazing things happened. There, everything belonged to me. Any marble statue, any Gothic cathedral, any painting of a sad Madonna. They were mine because of the love and admiration which they evoked in me. For a very long time I did not know where the Nike of Samothrace stood. I didn't care. Having once seen the triumphant spread of her wings, their wind was always behind me. It was within my power to remember her, to see her any minute. She was wherever I was.

Later I would never be surprised by greedy and jealous collectors who didn't want to exhibit their treasures. Of course! One glance, and the occasional viewer would become a co-owner. A piece could be put back then, and never shown again, but the viewer now remembered what he saw. Maybe even, more terribly, he saw in that one glance more than the real owner had ever seen. Who, then, was the owner? Everything was suddenly reversed!

I did not own a single shiny enameled clay pot like the dozen that Aunt Khvenya had. But I had alabaster vessels from the Egyptian pyramids, and Minoan plates with twisting octopi, red- and black-figure amphorae, hydras, and craters. On top of them feasting gods lounged, heroes fought, and triumphant marches proceeded. Or simply, a swallow flew into a room, where it astonished a young woman, a bearded man, and a boy. "Look, a swallow! Yes, it's true, I swear by Hercules—springtime is here!"

And all this treasure would make our poverty sink into the background somewhere. A Greek vase with a swallow—would I ever agree to exchange it for one of Aunt Khvenya's jugs that were drying on the fence under the sun? The jug was nice, reliable, and hardworking, but it knew only how to say, "Okay, I'm ready, where's the milk?" I liked it very much, but it couldn't compare to the vase with the swallow.

But that meant that we had everything most important and necessary, and all we lacked were "useless" things. Mama didn't have her own room, but she had a cool cave full of flowers in the stable. I had the vase with the spring swallow and so much more! I don't think either Mama or I was conscious of this. But in trying to understand why, in this spartan life, we never sensed ourselves cheated or slighted, why we may have sometimes felt unhappy but never oppressed or second-rate—I thought this was the explanation.

Strangely, while I sat with *Global History of the Arts,* and later with similar books, no compass was pointing me toward France, the country which would preoccupy me later for so many years. That was still far ahead. In Kuschevka I had already read *Ninety-three* and it had excited me. But not one thread linked it to those months ahead when I would write a book about Jacques-Louis David, consumed by the Convention's bulletins on the cherished bookshelves of Prince Lobanov-Rostovsky at the Hermitage library. There were no steppe roots in this passion. There were other roots, from a besieged Leningrad.

I remember well sitting in the Hermitage library, at the giant common mahogany table, in an armchair by the window facing Palace Square. I had just been brought a brochure printed in 1792, a document from the trial of Louis XVI. It was a tiny booklet, printed on rough paper. In spots the fat fibers, almost chips, bulged so sharply that the letters on them were hard to discern. I put my palm on this gray uneven paper, and suddenly a lucid, piercing feeling of something remote but unforgotten rose up in me. Of course. There it was. A slice of Blockade bread with wood fibers in it. An "eighth." My palm remembered before I did. And so I found myself in the middle of a triangle drawn around me, unimaginable and irrefutable. A starving, icy Leningrad in 1941. A starving, infuriated Paris two centuries ago. And the steppe, far away and buried under snowdrifts, books on our wooden table under a broiler lamp. There began a journey which took me years and kilometers, so that here, among the bookshelves of an imperial library, I could hold in my hands this brochure from the Convention, which closed all three sides of the triangle.

But this was still so far ahead!

Back then, I was delirious with the ancient eras. I knew mythology and Homer much better in my tenth year than I do now. The most powerful gods somehow did not attract me. The awesome and beautiful face of Zeus did not mesh with his deeds, or the strange stories in which he kept getting himself involved. I almost hated the gorgeous Apollo and Artemide for Niobe's children. I couldn't imagine young and mighty gods killing children before their mother's eyes. Their faces themselves seemed arrogant and icy to me.

But I passionately admired the simple, nameless, and magical demigods, and semi-people, who lived in the forests, rivers, and oceans. The fauns, the dryads, the nymphs, the Nereids, the tritons all seemed to be lighthearted souls. None of them would have killed innocent children in a fit of rage or vengeance. And it was their friendships with trees, springs, and sea waves that I envied.

I also envied the Amazons, who rode their horses fearlessly and unstoppably across the wild steppes. Imagine, maybe they galloped through this very valley to let their horses drink from the Yeia! I wanted so much to race with them through hot

winds, delirious with freedom and open space, my hair streaming behind me, my quiver slapping my side, and the bronze
rings of my bridle jingling.

But most of all I loved the story of the argonauts. I still
love it, and there is nothing surprising about that. It is one of
those stories that can accompany you through every age, and
during each you can open to the needed page. It is a story for
youth, when it is so easy to abandon all that is nearby for something faraway and unknown, for the sake of a beautiful legend
which vaguely promises something. When there is nothing happier than a sail above your head, a rocking deck under your feet,
and a hope for hurricanes and monsters. And all wishes come
true—storms, dragons, battles, love, magic, and miracles. But
the unwished happens too—betrayal, cruelty, losses, and broken oaths. Then the tide recedes further, taking others with it,
and you are left face-to-face with old age and emptiness. Actually, that's how it seems to Jason alone: for we know already
that the argonauts' lives became a legend and thus indispensable
to others—like me, two and a half thousand years later. Nothing passes. Nobody leaves.

Once when I was reading on the grass under the acacias,
some Cossack women from our brigade came and sat down beside me for one of their "salty snacks." During the heat, everybody would converge on our yard to rest and wait out the
most difficult hours. There was always lots of conversation
over a snack. What was I reading? they asked me. I was pleased
to be asked, and inspired to share my favorite story. So with all
my passion and pathos, I laid out the story of the argonauts

in all its detail. They listened carefully, with interest, but it did not make any special impression. Most of their questions concerned the value of the golden fleece: Was it worth it? I stressed Medea's horrible story in particular, thinking that women would identify strongly with this female tragedy. I was wrong. They felt no special compassion for Medea at all: "What a basket-case." Her excess of emotions was clearly alien to them. Very indignant, I delivered a rousing speech on her behalf. Once again, the result was unpredictable. The Cossack women chose not to argue with me about Medea, but unanimously approved that I spoke with such authority, as if it were in the book. "And what else do you know about these ancient men?"

Noticing that stories about travel and battles were best received, I began recounting the wanderings of Odysseus. Never again, at any conference or seminar with students, would I have such a wonderful audience! It was amazing to watch these stern and reclusive women, seemingly incapable of anything sentimental, become so transformed. Eyes shining, they would lower an unfinished slice of bread and lard to their knees, as each new trick by Odysseus would inspire a quiet admiration among them. Their expressions would become simple and open, the lines in their faces softening, revealing unbridled curiosity and compassion. The sirens kept singing, I told the ladies, but everyone's ears on the ship were stuffed with wax. Only Odysseus heard the magical singing, but he was tied to the mast. He was desperately tearing at the ropes so that he could leap to where the sirens were . . . "So why didn't he stuff his own ears?" "Didn't you hear her say, he wanted to hear the sirens singing, don't you get it?"

They would bend toward me, eager to hear. Not only did I never again have such an audience, I also never put forth such effort for my listeners—nowhere, not on the lectern of the Hermitage theatre hall, nor in a Moscow auditorium full of gray-haired academics and pitiless critics. Odysseus amazed everybody, slashing apart the most complex nets with precise strokes, hammering holes through the most invincible walls. He knew how to find Achilles, dressed as a girl, among Lycomedes' daughters. He knew how to shepherd his fellow travelers from the cave of the cannibal Polyphemus, and how to evade both Scylla and Charybdis at once. And Penelope kept waiting for him, weaving in the day and unweaving at night, believing that he would return. This the women could identify with, for almost all of them were also waiting and weaving. Somewhere, already far away from us, the war dragged on. We all understood that it would yet be lengthy and brutal. Here the Cossack ladies would lower their heads, retreat within themselves, and silently fidget with the folds on their skirts. And Penelope was raising Telemachos, waiting and weaving. And years went by.

From then on, this midday ritual would continue without fail. Each lunchtime, I would find myself among expectant listeners. They would either ask me to repeat yesterday's myth or clamor for a new one. Then they would ask to see my books, treating them very carefully and tenderly, examining the pictures: And who is this? And he? And she?

They were completely bewildered by the multitude of Greek gods and by Olympus' unstable pluralism, where irreconcilable interests clashed and gods interfered in each other's affairs. Later, I would notice among simple and independently thinking people this jealous attention to the purely human aspects of a foreign religion, as opposed to its canons. For them, a god's human nature was the nature of the religion itself. This struck me during an expedition to Svanetia. The Svans called themselves Christians, but all their rituals were heathenistic. They worshipped the sun, summoned the spirits of the dead, and in their main holy place was a huge sheep pen guarded by spears, filled with a pile of beautiful Caucasian goat horns (all sacrifices by the hunters). The Svans were suspicious of our work in their churches, as with anything to do with foreigners. But they were also respectful and clearly approving: They were flattered by it. Once, near Mestiya, two elderly Svans came up to me in a church. I was selected only because I was not photographing, measuring, or writing things down, but simply looking at the frescoes—in their view, doing nothing. Do you know gods? Yes. Is it true that Isa Krist is the supreme god? Yes. More supreme than Djgrag? And Tevdore? Yes.

They were staring at me suspiciously. Why is He supreme? I was not ready for this question, but I had to respond. He did the most for people. And He was the kindest one.

The mistrust in their gloomy eyes turned to disagreement. A stone wall. Unacceptable. This could not be true. Djgrag is on a horse, Djgrag has a sword, he is a warrior. Krist has none of that. How can He be more supreme? In this land, where even the adolescent boys who guided us through a mountain pass (where nothing threatened us at all) would sling rifles across their shoulders, an unarmed god could not be more supreme than an armed one. What could he do for people, without a horse or a sword?

My listeners, the Cossack ladies, from childhood were also used to seeing stern and sorrowful religious images. In the corner of a living room, where shutters were almost always closed, and cool semi-darkness reigned, the sense of the ceremonious heart of a home was universally preserved. There would be a bridal photo of Grandma with a cavalry officer of the Order of George standing by her chair, and photos of the head of household and sons who were off at the front. The most beautiful embroideries and the most expensive blankets were laid on the bed, and the best ancient pottery on a shelf or sideboard. But then a guest would see, higher than this heart, soaring above it, the icons with their sad eyes that knew all faults without confession. When I would happen to see—very rarely—our former landlady or Aunt Khvenya before an icon, they had identical facial expressions of shyness and subservience, unnatural for them. But how can you feel subservient before a multi-voiced crowd of Greek gods—passionate, vindictive, generous, petty, and sinful?

"And who's that fellow?," they would ask, pointing to a statue of Dionysus. I would explain in detail. "They even have a god for wine?" They were stunned. This in their eyes was an excess. But they clearly approved of Mercury and especially Demeter. The story of Persephone touched them more than that of Medea: "That isn't fair. She kept raising that baby, and then . . . " But Apollo, Artemide, and the Muses and Graces were treated with complete indifference.

Given my age, it was not surprising that I exhausted almost the entire population of Olympus before telling them about a goddess of love. And I had just barely mentioned her, not planning to go into the whole story. But the news that the Greeks had such a goddess nearly caused a volcanic eruption. The women would not even let me begin until the whole lunch crowd had gathered from all corners of the yard and hut. It was good that Nikifor Kondratich was not around—all his kind-heartedness toward us might not have survived had he learned why his brigade's lunch break was being extended.

And so, one quiet spring morning, the waves lapped at the shore of a Greek island, as always. The island was in the middle of a warm blue sea where dolphins splashed and played. Its shores were lined with soft sand, and higher in the hills grew olive trees. Higher still the mountains began, where sheep grazed in the pastures. And, as everywhere, dryads lived in the forests and Nereids in the water—just like our mermaids. Maybe there were many such islands in the warm Ionic Sea. But it was near this one that one day the oceanic foam began gathering near the cliffs, and bubbling under the sun as never before . . . (I had never seen the ocean and could only imagine the foam from a washbasin at laundry time.) And suddenly a beautiful young lady rose up out of the sea. She looked around and smiled. (I had only seen a poor reproduction of Botticelli's painting, in which it was impossible to tell that Venus, standing on the edge of a seashell, looked around herself with aloof sadness. Even so, at ten years of age, I could only have believed that Venus, stepping over the shining foam, must surely have been smiling—at the sea, the dolphins, the white columns, and her own beauty.)

Venus' marriage to Vulcan aroused much general anxiety and discussion. Did she do it voluntarily, or was it an arranged marriage? Was there no better man than a lame one? Okay, at least he wasn't a hunchback. But she was the prettiest one, and a goddess too! So how did they live?

It turned out that their life wasn't that good, and Mars' appearance on the scene was greeted with unanimous approval. Who would suit the prettiest goddess better than a brave soldier? Vulcan's jealous vigilance made everyone tense and nervous; the audience was divided. Some urged me to continue, but others wanted to give their opinions first. Since she's a goddess, she might as well have some fun! But what would have happened to a simple woman? Then some of the ladies stuck up for Vulcan. Why then did Venus marry him in the first place? And now that she had, she must endure! Some even cited Penelope as a role model for the unfaithful Venus.

But when Venus and Mars were trapped in the crafty Vulcan's net, I was puzzled again. A flood of unbridled mirth assailed me from all sides. Everybody, regardless of age or personality, laughed uncontrollably. Gloating? No, nothing like it. Sympathy for Vulcan? Also no. Actually yes, but not for him alone. They sympathized with all three at once: "They're gods but they've got the same troubles as people!" And since they were people—ordinary, sinful, and simple—there was this explosion of understanding, forgiveness, and cheerful humor. Things I had never witnessed among these reclusive and inexpressive women before. Here and there, someone was still disapproving of somebody, someone was happy, but all together this noisy party did not want to condemn or sentence, only to understand.

No matter how much separated us from the Cossack women at first, they very soon had begun to evoke in me a feeling of involuntary respect and approval. Even in arguments with them, everything was clear, firm, and open. I accepted their straight shoulders and unswerving eyes; the firm nature of their opinions and their straightforward manner of expressing them as basic societal norms. I hadn't begun to fathom that in our day and age, this kind of decent conduct remained on only a few scattered islands of civilization. And that I had just happened to stumble across one of these islands. I was still far from understanding that all this had a name—internal freedom. My notions about freedom then were totally different—childish and bookish. In them, it was pure and obvious, perched on a pedestal of nobility. Yet, I would have sooner recognized the Cossack women's freedom if they had not looked at me indifferently while I lay emaciated and helpless across a threshold. If they had not closed their doors to me and Mama when we were retreating from the Germans through the steppe. If they had not taken our last dresses and Grandfather's cross in exchange for a little bag of flour or a stick of lard. They had so much in their basements and ice chests anyway. Or did it just seem that way to me after the Leningrad famine?

It was impossible then for me to understand that the same feeling could be expressed in opposite ways. Mama and I, like those Cossack women, treasured independence above all. But to us, this meant that we must submit ourselves to many deprivations. I would overhear shreds of conversation between Mama and Father about meetings where someone had renounced a friend, or husband, or even brother. "All for their sorry careers . . ." Mama would say. Her voice was harsh, even merciless, as never before. I knew the words but couldn't understand what they meant. Your career was your job, and to renounce meant to deny any connection. But how is someone's brother connected to one's job? And how can you deny your connection to him, since he never stopped being your brother? Grandma would talk about someone who lived in poverty, but had remained an honest person and so his conscience, thank God, was at peace. "To live in poverty" and "to remain an honest person" somehow kept growing closer. Poverty was becoming something honorable and respectable. You just had to get used to denying yourself various things. Mama would often reply to Yelizaveta Nikolayevna's urgings to barter longer with the Cossack women: "Why, do these rags really mean anything? I'm happy that it represents value to them. And so we too now have food for a week ahead. A whole week of life!"

But to the Cossack women, our things really did represent value. Precisely because they too treasured independence. But to them it meant that the home had to be fully stocked, for the coming year and beyond. Because poverty meant begging someone for something, becoming indebted, becoming someone's servant. Poverty is dependence. When the chests and the basement were full, that was true freedom.

It's a great gift to people that, aside from the usual senses, they also have a constantly working intuition. Better than human reason, it knows where among the mud is a place for a straight road, where instead of a thick wall an open spot must be—and it lays the road and dismantles the wall. And so it was with us. By all signs, we should not have agreed on anything with the farm women from the vegetable-garden brigade. But we befriended each other, despite it all. We were learning, and we finally learned, to discern our real sisterhood beneath our unaccommodating appearances, beneath our reclusive alienation. (How often, later in adult life, the reverse would happen. My child's intuition would be forgotten, and I would trust in words and appearances. And meanwhile a person who was saying the same things as I was would write reports about me to the KGB.)

When I tried later to remember what triggered the turnaround in our relations, it finally came to me. Having survived the occupation and looking back at it, we had suddenly realized: No one had betrayed us. Not one of the Germans who visited the vegetable-garden brigade seemed to suspect that anybody lived there, let alone two Leningrad families, including the wife and daughter of a combat officer and a Communist. Not one of their guides had told them anything. And it would have been so easy to butter up an annoyed guest with a sudden revelation.

Why did the local people want us to survive? We were aliens by birth, by our whole way of life, and most of all by our ideology. They awaited the Germans as allies. Why then, visiting our yard with the Germans, did they act as our allies?

I asked Mama about this. Her tone indicated that my question was not unexpected. Nonetheless she replied not with an explanation but rather with another question.

"Do you remember how much they were cursing the Soviet regime right in front of us? We didn't like it. But now, would you go to the authorities and report how they talked? Would you point them out with your finger?"

"Me?" I got scared. "No! Never!"

"All right then," said Mama.

Picking up an empty bucket from the bench, she walked out into the yard.

This meant that the rest was for me to figure out myself.

I tried with all my might, but my might was insufficient. I did not even understand the answer I had just blurted out. Indeed, why would I not go? For our duty was, actually, to expose fearlessly. So how could it be good that I would not go, that I did not *want* to go and report them?

Here my little thoughts would begin to stumble. The only clear thing in this whole mess was that it had turned out we and the Cossacks were somehow alike. They did not want to betray us. And we would not want to betray them. But weren't we vastly different? So this meant that our differences were not the most important thing. Then what was?

I suddenly felt as if I still had to travel a very long and difficult road. But there is nothing better or simpler than a road—just keep on walking, doubting nothing, stopping nowhere, with the sun shining above you. This, however, was another kind of road, and nothing was simple here. An unfamiliar fear was creeping up on me—you can go astray, or not reach your final destination, or simply get lost somewhere without ever having understood anything. And my awareness of the necessity of this trip was far from being light and happy. Yet it was impossible to avoid. Why did the Cossacks never betray us, and why would we never betray them?

Suddenly the door swung open and Nirs burst in, barely catching his breath.

"Mikola's driving hay to the fruit-garden brigade, and he says we can come too! They've got apples there—he says we should bring a bucket. Come on!"

SITTING IN THE CIRCLE of my grown-up Cossack lady friends, I was absorbing deeper and deeper their strong and sweeping love of life, their skill of breathing with a full chest and of stubbornly holding their ground. Our hard-earned kinship did not have the simplicity and openness which exists in an immediate and happy friendship between people who understand each other from the first word. But something, perhaps precisely this difficulty, made it more valuable to us. It did not fall on us from the sky like a gift. We built it, with our own hands, with long dirty work. Month after month we cleared away the mountains of incomprehension and prejudice that had been piled up between us. We understood something very important, and learned something very necessary, by doing this work.

This was a light and happy time. We were finally locals here. After long months of tension, alienation, and orientation, we had been, at last, accepted.

But very soon a change was to occur. Not with me and Mama, but for us it was a reminder that changes were only beginning, and that some things in our lives might, or even must, shift. And our recently acquired feeling of stability became shaky.

Yelizaveta Nikolayevna's husband came to take her and the children back to Leningrad. I do not quite remember what their situation was. Apparently he had not been at the front at all, but worked at some secret factory which was exempt from the draft. Somehow the Blockade found him outside Leningrad, and so it happened that the family was evacuated without him. I hardly remember him at all, except that he seemed like an uncommonly mellow and contented person for those times. Perhaps it was the way he walked around the yard and the hut itself, looking about with cheerful and condescending perplexity, like a white man who finds himself in a tribal village. Following his gaze, I saw, as if for the first time, the cracks in our ceiling and the stains of peeled paint on the walls. So what? I was insulted on behalf of our hut. But by then I was definitely not a white person. I was a tribal girl.

Aunt Khvenya immediately proclaimed that now Mama and I would really live it up—a whole room for the two of us! But somehow this did not cheer us up. True, we had not been that close to Yelizaveta Nikolayevna's family. She and Mama were very different people, and for me Dagmara was too big, almost an adult, and Nirs was too small. But we had held our friendship together during the most difficult times. We shared in our past that deadly train, and the Blockade before that. This formed a strong bond. And we sat together at our table during those long winter nights, snowstorms pounding our windows, reading Pushkin and Gogol under the broiler lamp. This was also kinship, and what a kinship it was!

Now, in a happy frenzy, they were packing their things. I could have envied them. But strangely for me there was something alien, almost offensive in their joy. What if Mama and I were able to go back to Leningrad too? So far this was impossible, for it remained a closed city. You had to have close relatives there and we had nobody left. Or you had to receive a special "invitation," co-signed by the city government, confirming that for some reason you were needed there. But if we could go, would I be celebrating like this too? I could not imagine so.

Mama had been at work in the fields since morning. I did

not want to disturb Yelizaveta Nikolayevna's happy packing. So I shoved a piece of bread and a tomato into my pocket, and headed off to the steppe. It is strange, or maybe not strange at all, that on that day I set out on a route I rarely took. I followed the road—that same one, from the starry night—then passed the field of sunflowers, not paying them a visit this time, and then turned at the divide and walked left, until the field ended and the railroad now stretched before me.

On the way to Kuschevka, there was a tiny rail station, really just a stop—Chernomorka. A line branched off from the railroad there, and headed south to the Black Sea. Our closest neighbors were here as well. There were two or three small houses, as I recall, where former railroad workers lived. I loved walking there when the ancient sprawling acacias were in bloom. They were such huge, aromatic trees, and their dense shade such a rarity in the steppe that it seemed I had ended up in another country.

I kept walking. Now Chernomorka was far behind me. Looking back, I saw only the tops of the trees. There was nothing and nobody around me. I stood alone on an abandoned rail line. Winter-cress bushes with bright yellow flowers had grown up between the tie beams. The rails had grown unaccustomed to trains, but still remembered them. Here, among the familiar scents of the hot steppe soil and blossoming herbs, some other totally foreign odor was breaking through. It could have been the hot old lubrication grease of the rails, scorched under the sun, or the wooden ties soaked with petroleum that had spilled and dried up long ago. It was a strange and worrisome smell.

Tomorrow Yelizaveta Nikolayevna would leave. We would stay behind. Would we stay? I already knew that the answer was no. I felt no happiness about this. I even felt sorry to think that I would lose my steppe. But the harsh discipline of the war years had taught me the words "necessary" and "no choice" very early. Yelizaveta Nikolayevna's departure was a warning about our own departure—in a half-year, or two years, perhaps, but it was bound to happen. There was no choice. This I knew.

The war was still raging, and we were at the mercy of its underground tremors, invisible yet cataclysmic in scope. One of them had thrown us here into the steppe. Now a return wave was approaching, growing closer. And I was already standing on a road, over which no trains passed anymore. But it remained a road that came from somewhere and went to somewhere. I stood on this road as if here I might understand more clearly: Where? When? How will it all end?

But nothing was made clearer. The road and everything around it were deserted. The wind here, on this open plain, was stronger than in the steppe. To the right of me sunflowers were rocking their heads, to the left of me light waves of feather-grass swayed. The wind came from the south, and for some reason I began to walk into it.

I knew nothing about anything. The future appeared to me as a clean sheet of paper, without a single mark on it. But all the co-authors of my fate had already agreed on everything: Grandfather's portrait, and my childhood without school; *Global History of the Arts*, and the snowstorms which spun outside our window as we read by the broiler lamp; the Blockade of

Leningrad, and the summer steppe road under a starry night. Everything had been foretold.

About all this I only knew one thing: There would be a farewell to the steppe, and another new road. That's what I was testing now, the road, stepping slowly over beams covered with grass.

All right then, I was ready.

ABOUT THE AUTHOR

Elena Kozhina was born in Moscow and spent most of her childhood in Leningrad. After earning her Ph.D. in art history at Leningrad State University, she spent more than twenty years at the Hermitage, where she curated the Old French paintings collection and published two books and numerous articles. In 1984, she emigrated to the United States with her husband and son. She wrote *Through the Burning Steppe* in tribute to her mother's heroism and as a legacy for her son, who translated the work. Kozhina lives with her family in New York City.

ABOUT THE TRANSLATOR

Vadim Mahmoudov translated his mother's book into English in 1998. An attorney in New York City, he is fluent in English, Russian, and French.

Discussion Questions for
THROUGH THE BURNING STEPPE

. The power of memory is a recurring theme in *Through the Burning Steppe*. How does memory both weaken and strengthen the women in the story?

. While living in the hut on the steppe, Elena discovers that books provide momentary escape from the horrors of her situation. However, she often finds that the words she reads remind her of the tragic things she has experienced in her young life. Do you think literature can provide true solace, or does it merely offer an escape? Why does Kozhina draw such comfort from her books? Is there a common theme to the types of stories she is drawn to repeatedly?

. Elena is forced to make sacrifices and life-and-death choices at an early age, and in some sense, is deprived of a carefree childhood. Compare Kozhina's story to other accounts of children who are forced to grow up too soon (consider the works of Anne Frank, Jerzy Kosinski, Elie Wiesel, Kenzaburo Oe, Gunter Grass, etc.). Do you think Kozhina was a particularly resourceful child? Can you identify a single factor as most important to Kozhina's survival?

. Why does the German soldier who searches Elena's hut have trouble reconciling the photograph of her father wearing an Orthodox Christian robe with the fact that he is a Communist? Elena reflects that had the soldier performed the search a year later, he would not have hesitated in killing Elena and her mother because he would have been "hardened" by the war. In what ways is Elena both hardened by the effects of the war and simultaneously made more sensitive and generous by the years spent on the steppe?

. What does Elena's mother do to help Elena stave off her fits of despair? From what do you think Elena's mother draws the strength to carry on herself?

6. With time, Elena begins taking journeys into the steppe to explore its many beauties. She describes the countryside as a "generous" world where "there were no incurable wounds or unfulfillable dreams." Can you think of an instance in your life where you were inspired by or drew strength or hope from nature? Kozhina describes the nature around her as "beautiful," but what other qualities can be attributed to her depiction of the surrounding countryside?

7. In her awakening to art, Elena realizes that beauty—and the desire to make things beautiful—is as necessary to humans as food or shelter. Do you agree with this? Do you think the desire to create art can be called instinctual?

8. The Cossack women Elena and her mother befriend may be uneducated, but one can argue that they are also far less naïve than the Leningraders, and that these women offer an education of their own. How does Elena's perception of government change after spending time with the Cossack women? Do you think she also evaluates people differently than she might had she never lived in the steppe?

9. To her surprise and delight, Kozhina finds that the Cossack women have a great appetite for the Greek myths she tells them on their lunch breaks. Why do you think the women had such an enthusiastic response to these stories? What does their reaction say about their definition of heroism? How does that definition differ from Kozhina's own?

10. In the course of this memoir, Elena Kozhina makes some allusions to her career as an art historian at the Hermitage, where she suffered intellectual persecution from her colleagues and superiors alike. In the end, do you think Kozhina actually experienced more freedom as a child during wartime than as an adult under a Communist regime? What did Kozhina's childhood experiences in the steppe teach her about personal liberties and freedom?

11. In one of the final lines of her memoir, Elena declares, "I knew nothing about anything." Is this declaration surprising, considering all she has learned about life and death at such a young age? How is Elena, by the end of the story, both very young and very old at the same time?

2/02 12
8/03 - 15